PAGAN AND CHRISTIAN EGYPT

PAGAN AND CHRISTIAN EGYPT

EGYPTIAN ART FROM THE FIRST
TO THE TENTH CENTURY A. D.

Exhibited at the Brooklyn Museum

by the Department of Ancient Art

January 23—March 9

1941

BROOKLYN MUSEUM

BROOKLYN INSTITUTE *of* ARTS *and* SCIENCES

1941

Copyright 1941

BROOKLYN INSTITUTE OF ARTS AND SCIENCES

BROOKLYN MUSEUM

Library of Congress Catalog Card No. 69-17449

ISBN 0-913696-25-0

Second Reprint 1974

PRODUCED FOR THE BROOKLYN MUSEUM
BY THE PUBLISHING CENTER FOR CULTURAL RESOURCES
MANUFACTURED IN THE UNITED STATES OF AMERICA

To
Charles Edwin Wilbour
a pioneer American egyptologist
who early showed an interest in
the closing chapters of
ancient Egyptian civilization
and whose collection in the
Brooklyn Museum
forms the nucleus
of this exhibition

Pagan and Christian Egypt

O N THE EVE of the first century of the Christian era, Egypt no longer possessed the cultural unity which had been so striking a characteristic of her history throughout the Pharaonic period.   Even before the Ptolemaic occupation of the country late in the fourth century B.C., Egypt had shown signs of a cultural disintegration, which was aided by the various foreign invasions previous to the conquest of Alexander the Great. The invasions left little, if any, trace on the art of Egypt.   Greek influence made a brilliant impression, but it penetrated only the Delta and hardly touched Upper Egypt, which clung to the decaying tradition of Pharaonic art.   A sharp division must therefore be made between the productions of Upper and Lower Egypt during the Ptolemaic period.   With the coming of the Romans, shortly before the time of Christ, political unity was once more achieved, but in art the result of the Roman conquest was simply the introduction of one more discordant element.   Egypt was in cultural chaos, a situation from which she was not to emerge until at least the late fourth century, when, under the influence of the Coptic Church, she once more attained unity of art expression.   It is with this era of political unity and cultural confusion, culminating in Coptic art, that this exhibition deals.

From the conflicting trends of the first two centuries after Christ, three main currents in the art of Egypt can be separated:

     1.   Survivals of the Egyptian style.
     2.   Greek (Hellenistic) work.
     3.   Roman work.

Of these elements, the least important, though perhaps the most persistent, is work in the Egyptian style.   With the breaking down of a native centralized power and the dependence of the still influential priesthood on the Greek Court in Alexandria, the royal studios had disappeared. Gradually, during the earlier part of the Ptolemaic period, the native Egyptian upper classes likewise vanished, and thus patronage in traditional Egyptian objects survived only among the poor. It is for this reason that we find so very few objects in Egyptian style after the time of Christ. Funerary stelae, usually of poor workmanship, form by far the largest class of surviving objects. Sculpture in the round is extremely rare. Conventional temple reliefs, usually portraying the Roman Emperors among the Egyptian gods, survive in a dead and archaistic style. Even in so minor a field as jewelry only occasionally are specimens found in the purely Egyptian tradition. Statuettes of composite deities abound; they bear witness to the feebleness of Egyptian craftsmen in the absence of a centralized native power. In short, the native Egyptian art of this period presents only weak survivals.

Greek art was always foreign to Egyptian taste, and it is doubtful if many of the pieces in the Greek style surviving from the Ptolemaic period were made for native use. The religion and mental processes of the Alexandrian Greeks were so alien to the Egyptian temperament that once the Ptolemaic Court collapsed, productions of first class workmanship almost ceased. The numerous remains of Greek work, coming usually from Lower and Middle Egypt, give evidence of the persistence of earlier traditions among the Greek population. The Fayum portraits are an excellent example of this class of work. They were undoubtedly descended from Hellenistic painting, but gradually they achieved a style of their own, finally merging into Coptic. Greek influence is particularly obvious in many of the crafts, such as ceramics and bone carving. Possibly the centers of production for such objects were in Greek cities, but we know too little of such matters to be certain. So little has survived in Alexandria that our knowledge of the output of the city during the period is precarious. It seems safe to infer that the Greek tradition must have survived there. It was certainly the center for most of the wealthier and well educated Greek-speaking people of Egypt. Most of the surviving objects in the Greek style come from the small Greek colonies south of the Delta and show all of the characteristics typical of provincial work.

The influence of Roman work is not apparent until well into the first century. The Roman style seems to have appealed to Egypt much more than the Greek, and most Roman sculptures from Egypt show a mingling of Roman and Egyptian elements. Sculpture in the round, usually portraits, is dry and hard, frequently archaistic but rarely lacking in vigor. Hard stones were commonly employed instead of the soft limestone used in the contemporary Egyptian reliefs and smaller Greek sculptures. A large part of the gold work of the period is in the Roman style, frequently combined with traditional Egyptian motifs. The use of such motifs does not indicate any real fusion of styles. Usually they seem little more than an elaborate way of marking the object "Made in Egypt". The Roman style can fairly be called the dominant style of Egypt during the first two centuries.

The third century in Egypt is not very clear. Speaking generally, it does not seem to have been productive, and certainly, with the heavy taxation imposed on Egypt, the growing poverty of the country and the decline of Roman power, one would not expect great productivity. After the early part of the third century, hard stone is rarely found in large sculptures, the head of Caracalla in the University Museum, Philadelphia, being one of the latest examples of colossal sculpture in hard stone. It is frequently stated that sculptures in hard stone dating from the third century are never found. Certainly they were not common, but some of the heads in this exhibition are of hard stone and may well belong to the third century. They show some kinship with the famous porphyry sculptures in Cairo, generally dated as about 300 A. D. Undoubtedly numerous stelae were produced and some gold work can be dated with certainty to the third century. It is hard to state that any particular style predominates in the third century. Future studies may justify the use of the term Proto-Coptic for this period.

Included in the exhibition is a selection of terra cottas, most of which date from the second to the fourth century. These are interesting chiefly as documents of the synthetic religion of the Roman Empire, which found expression in Egypt, sometimes in a combination of native Egyptian with Greek and Oriental deities, sometimes in deities with scarcely a trace of Egyptian origin. These little terra cottas are, for the most part, poor in quality. They may in some instances be copies of cult images, now lost, which existed in the temples of Alexandria and other centers. They were undoubtedly products of mass production, souvenirs and *objets de piété* from the homes of the humble. Some of them may have been votive objects deposited at shrines. While it is difficult, if not impossible, to establish an exact date for them, the consensus of opinion is that most of them are of the late Imperial period. They may be taken as evidence of the cultural chaos that marked the decline of the Roman power and civilization in Egypt.

Added evidence is furnished by coins of the Roman period, which frequently show cult representations. Thanks to Mr. Edward C. Newell of the American Numismatic Society, who has made for us selections from

7

his private collection, we are able to show a number of these coins in photographic enlargement. Most of them date from the second century.

The rise of Christianity cannot be traced in art productions of the first three centuries. Certainly the Christian element in Egypt was already strong by the end of the third century, but it does not seem to have developed an art expression of its own. Objects made for the use of Christians apparently followed the traditional forms common in the community.

With the rise of the fourth century we are on somewhat more certain ground. Though almost nothing in this exhibition is dated in the catalogue as of this century, many of the pieces here listed as of the fifth century may as well belong to the fourth. Possibly the greater unity of expression found in this century is due in part to the Christianization of Egypt; there was no political or material event of sufficient importance to effect a change in the cultural life of the country. But a more probable explanation is that the native and foreign populations of Egypt had by now amalgamated and thus were competent to produce a more unified art expression. Purely Christian subjects are extremely rare, but Greek and Roman sculptures have ceased to exist, and already the funerary stelae show stylistic changes which bring them very close to what we know as Coptic art. The same tendencies are to be observed in painting; a good example is the Fayum portrait from the collection of Dr. Valentiner. The stela of Chairemon in the Brooklyn Collection shows, in its frontality and many of its details, renderings characteristic of Coptic art. It is in this period that the real beginnings of Coptic art must be traced, excluding, of course, the earlier Greek and Syrian elements that also determine the final evolution of this style.

At the very outset of any discussion of Coptic art there is the difficulty of determining the scope and meaning of the term Coptic. In its original meaning Coptic was applied to the Egyptian Christians. Today we use this theological classification as the designation of a style. In this catalogue many objects are termed Coptic which have no Christian association. Such attributions, made on stylistic grounds, can sometimes be applied as early as the second century, although no Christian objects from Egypt of this time are known. The terminology is none too satisfactory, but it is now so well established that it is useless to attempt to change it.

The origins of Coptic art are too complex and as yet too uncertain to discuss in this place. Any survey, however casual, of the objects in this exhibition will show that many trends are discernible in Coptic productions. In part these may be due to local variations but in great part they represent the various elements—Ancient Egyptian, Greek, Roman, Near

Eastern—which merge to form Coptic art. At the present time it is impossible to trace the geographical distribution of Coptic art within Egypt at any given period. As always, provincial work may represent the survival of an earlier style from one of the larger cities.

Coptic art produced few spectacular achievements. It is primarily a decorative art; it does not show great spiritual or philosophical insight. Its repertoire was not large. Constantly we find the same motifs repeated on stone, fabrics, pottery and ivories. The Coptic artist did not suit his design to the medium. All surfaces, whatever their substance, were filled with designs chosen without regard for the limitations of the medium. With this aim the greatest achievements of the Copts were in fresco painting and fabrics. The latter are well represented in the exhibition, but of the fresco painting there is no example. In this country, outside of the Morgan manuscripts here exhibited, the only representative Coptic paintings are the two splendid book covers in the Freer Gallery of Art in Washington, (see Morey, C. R., *East Christian Paintings in the Freer Collection*, New York, MacMillan, 1918. Univ. of Mich. Studies, Humanistic Series, v. 12). The stone reliefs, however, were frequently pictorial in style, and appear always to have been painted in color. In his excavations at the monastery of Apa Jeremias at Sakkara, Quibell found vine-leaf capitals painted in brilliant red and blue on a yellow ground. The relief from Pratt Institute apparently retains its original color, and traces of the same maroon-red were discovered under microscopic examination on the reliefs of St. Thekla and St. Sisinnios in the Brooklyn Collection. The reliefs with floral and vine motifs were probably decorated in the same manner.

So completely was the decorative purpose uppermost in Coptic art that the Copts did not scruple to incorporate into the decorated portions of their buildings sculptured stones from Pharaonic tombs. Several reliefs from Old Kingdom mastabas were found by Quibell built into the facade of a chapel at Sakkara and the effect was quite pleasing. The logical medium for the Copts would have been mosaic, where vast, flat spaces were available for impressive designs in glowing colors. Had Coptic art developed along the line of Byzantine art, as it gave promise of doing, mosaic probably would have achieved great development. So far as I am aware no Coptic mosaics are known; although tesserae were found at the monastery of Apa Jeremias, apparently dating from the fourth century, the design could not be reconstructed.

Purely Christian subjects are infrequent in Coptic art before the sixth century and are not common until the seventh. The explanation probably is that classical mythology and history formed so traditional a

9

background that it was instinctive to draw on these subjects for figural representation. When the Copts drew on Christian history for subject matter it was first customary to select individual saints or the Virgin and Child for representation. In the sixth century more complex compositions are found and from then on the development of purely Christian representation was rapid. Various attempts have been made to read a Christian interpretation into the pagan scenes so frequently found in earlier Coptic art. It is very doubtful if these attempts are justified. The Copts were probably portraying scenes familiar to them and their ancestors for many generations and a new art grammar had not arisen.

Sculpture in the round from the Coptic period hardly exists today. A few small pieces are included in the exhibition. There are perhaps no more than a few others in the country, outstanding among them the painted plaster figure in the Metropolitan Museum. In part this rarity is due to accident. Early in the eighth century the Arabs destroyed all the Coptic paintings and sculptures they could locate, and this was but the first of many attacks on Coptic property. Undoubtedly a certain number of sculptures in the round existed, but they were probably never very common. With their decorative point of view, the Copts had little feeling for three-dimensional sculpture and it probably did not appeal to their taste. While there was nothing in Christianity to prohibit the use of sculptures, the common use of them by the pagan religions and the associations with the multitudes then surviving from the Pharaonic period, must have prejudiced the Copts against them.

In the minor arts and handicrafts, the level of workmanship is not high. In comparison with the productions of the earlier Egyptian craftsmen and of contemporary and later craftsmen in other Mediterranean cities, Coptic crafts are not of outstanding quality. Perhaps it was because the Copts were interested primarily in the general effect and not in perfection of detail. Or perhaps many of the finer pieces have been lost, victims of Arab depredation. Exceptionally, bronze casting retained a high level. Some of these bronzes show Syrian influence but there is no reason to suppose they were made outside of Egypt. The absence of the royal court and the establishment of Constantinople doubtless drew the best craftsmen of Alexandria to the new royal city, and it was inevitable that Egyptian products would bear a somewhat provincial air.

Coptic art well merits study and a richer representation in American collections. Its connection with the earliest years of Christianity and the large and representative selection surviving would alone justify a study were justification necessary. The old attitude that Coptic art, along with Roman art, was little more than a bastard descendant of late anti-

quity has yielded to the obvious truth that the Copts developed an expression of their own. To some extent this new art was part of an international style common throughout the Mediterranean area from Spain to Syria. Borrowing, as have all cultures, from their predecessors, the Copts achieved an unmistakable individuality suited to new conditions. Doubtless Coptic art will never be classified as one of the great art periods, yet, it has characteristics which make it impressive. Its decorative qualities are obvious and it is never lacking in vigor. The Copts were clearly never greatly troubled by doubts, theological or philosophical, and this conviction rings in their art. As already stated, the repertoire of Coptic art was limited, but within its limitations there was tremendous variation. A study of value to scholars and designers could be made of the variants of the grapevine motif alone. A comparative study of Coptic motifs and those found on Nubian pottery might well assist in assigning a more exact date to Nubian burials. Irrespective of any direct connection, Coptic art possesses many of the elements common to Romanesque art and is of great value in a study of early Medieval art. The Coptic basilicas are excellent examples of the spirit common to the two cultures. With their dim interiors lit by windows made of small colored glass fragments set in plaster frames, their walls covered with blazing frescoes and ornate marble facings covering the transennae, they must have approached the Romanesque churches of Western Europe in general effect. Many of the reliefs, particularly those of the fifth and early sixth century, show cutting just as fine as the best Hellenistic work and a representation similar to Romanesque reliefs.

It is in the hope that Coptic studies will be stimulated that this exhibition has been assembled. Falling, as it does, between the fields of the Egyptologist and the Medievalist, the period has not been so thoroughly studied as might be supposed. Innumerable problems of iconography remain to be solved. Stylistic changes are very incompletely mapped. A coordinated study of the textiles and reliefs, in particular, as compared with similar objects in other cultures of the same period would undoubtedly enlarge our knowledge. At the present time, anyone wishing to catalogue Coptic jewelry, to mention only one field, has no comprehensive work to which he can refer. A careful study of reliefs and textiles would provide a large corpus of examples of jewelry. The interrelationship of decoration on all Coptic objects would make of general use even methodical study of one limited subject. Unfortunately, few persons possess the comprehensive knowledge of Hellenistic, later Near Eastern, and early Medieval art essential to any profound study of Coptic art.

So many persons have cooperated with the Museum in assembling this exhibition that it is difficult to give precedence to any single individual. Perhaps Mrs. Rudolf M. Riefstahl, of the Wilbour Library, has contributed most. The exhibition was originally conceived by her, and she has not only undertaken the entire task of assembling and cataloguing the textiles, but has also participated extensively in the balance of the exhibition. Prof. Lehmann-Hartleben, of New York University, has made many helpful suggestions and has assisted constantly in making selections for the exhibition. Mr. Marvin Chauncey Ross, of the Walters Art Gallery, pointed out many objects not previously known to the Museum and has assisted in attributions. Miss Elizabeth Dow, of the Dumbarton Oaks Collection, generously placed at the disposal of the Museum her notes on Christian objects in the United States. Mrs. Blanche Brown of New York likewise gave the Museum access to her notes on examples of ancient painting in this country. The very efficient W. P. A. organization at the Museum has made the labels and the posters for the exhibition and has assisted in preparing the manuscript of the catalogue for the printer.

To the many lenders who made possible this first American exhibition of Coptic art, the Brooklyn Museum acknowledges its indebtedness and expresses its gratitude. Several of the lenders were so kind as to offer pieces unknown to the Museum. Particular thanks are due Mr. George Hewitt Myers of Washington for consenting to strip his galleries of many of his choicest Coptic textiles for the duration of the Brooklyn exhibition. The generosity of the trustees of the Walters Art Gallery, and of the Mayor and City Council of the City of Baltimore in authorizing the loan of important and fragile objects, was a most important contribution to this exhibition. From the newly opened Dumbarton Oaks Collection have come interesting early objects. The cooperation of the Metropolitan Museum of Art and of Cooper Union Museum has added greatly to the exhibition, particularly in outstanding examples of textiles. Pratt Institute, under the very friendly cooperation of Mr. Frederic B. Pratt, transferred their entire Coptic collection to the Museum to facilitate the final selection for the exhibition. Last, but by no means least, this exhibition owes much to the art trade of New York City. The Brummer, Kevorkian and Kelekian galleries have provided interesting pieces, some of them outstanding. The Minassian collection has contributed notable textiles.

In the catalogue every attempt has been made to give bibliographical references. Inevitably some of the uses of the term 'unpublished' must be incorrect and indicate only that the compilers were unaware of any published account of the object. With a few exceptions complete bibliographies are not given. When a choice was possible, reference has been made to the more readily available work. Concerning measurements, the first measurement given is always the height.   As every object in the exhibition is presumably from Egypt, this fact is not listed under provenance.   The dates assigned are those of the compilers, and, in the majority of cases, they are only approximate.   Unquestionably a closer study will justify many changes in the dating here adopted.

John D. Cooney
Curator of Egyptology

PAINTING

*1. **FAYUM PORTRAIT ON WOOD OF AN UNKNOWN MAN.** Encaustic. Graeco-Egyptian. Late 1st-early IInd Century. .325 x .154 m.
PROVENANCE: Unknown.
BIBLIOGRAPHY: Stout, George L., *Technical Studies*, Vol. I, No. 2, Cambridge, 1932, pp. 82-93.
LENT BY: *Goucher College, Baltimore.*

*2. **FAYUM PORTRAIT ON WOOD OF THE LADY DEMETRIS.** Encaustic. Graeco-Egyptian. First half of IInd Century. .373 x .205 m.
PROVENANCE: Roman cemetery at Hawara.
BIBLIOGRAPHY: Petrie, W. F., *Roman Portraits and Memphis* IV, London, 1911, Pl. XXI; *Hawara Portfolio*, London, 1913, Pl. XII.
Brooklyn Museum Collection.

The mummy from which this portrait was taken is also in the Brooklyn Museum Collection. In spite of the masculine appearance of this portrait, it is apparently of a Lady Demetris whose name and age (eighty-nine) are recorded on the cartonnage.

*3. **FAYUM PORTRAIT ON WOOD OF AN UNKNOWN MAN.** Encaustic. Graeco-Egyptian. Second half of IInd Century. .36 x .185 m.
PROVENANCE: Unknown. Formerly in the collection of Howard Carter.
BIBLIOGRAPHY: Unpublished.
Brooklyn Museum Collection.

The gilded laurel wreath is conventional but here the cartonnage, of which fragments remain, was also gilded, at least around the portrait.

*4. **FAYUM PORTRAIT OF A MAN.** Gilt lips and laurel wreath. Encaustic on wood. Late IIIrd Century. Coptic. .369 x .191 m.
PROVENANCE: Said to be from Syria but certainly from Egypt.
BIBLIOGRAPHY: Unpublished.
LENT BY: *Dumbarton Oaks Collection.*

---

* Illustrated

*5. **FAYUM PORTRAIT OF A LADY.** Tempera on wood. Coptic. First half of IVth Century. .324 x .191 m.

PROVENANCE: Unknown.

BIBLIOGRAPHY: Drerup, H., *Datierung der Mummienporträts*, 1933, p. 44 & 62, Pl. 17A.

LENT BY: *Fogg Art Museum, Harvard University.*

*6. **FAYUM PORTRAIT OF A YOUNG LADY.** Tempera on wood. The right hand clasps a cup, the left a garland (?). Coptic. Early IVth Century. .302 x .194 m.

PROVENANCE: Unknown.

BIBLIOGRAPHY: Reinach, A., *Revue archaeologique*, 1915 (II), p. 17, Fig. 14.; Drerup, H., *Datierung der Mummienporträts*, 1933, p. 65, No. 33, Fig. 20.

LENT BY: *Dr. W. R. Valentiner.*

*7. **ICON OF THE GOD HERON (?) ON HORSEBACK,** grasping a double axe in his right hand. Tempera on wood. Egypto-Coptic. Early IIIrd Century. .369 x .183 m.

PROVENANCE: Said to be from the Fayum.

BIBLIOGRAPHY: Unpublished. For a discussion of the type see Cumont, F., Un dieu supposé syrien associé a Heron en Egypte, in *Mélanges syriens offerts à M. R. Dussaud.*

LENT BY: *Wadsworth Atheneum.*

8. **MALE PORTRAIT HEAD** on linen. Tempera. Probably from a large decorated shroud. Egyptian. IInd Century. .483 x .303 m.

PROVENANCE: Unknown.

BIBLIOGRAPHY: Unpublished.

LENT BY: *Fogg Art Museum, Harvard University.*

*9. **PAINTED CARTONNAGE.** Moulded and painted wreath on head. In right hand, a cup; in left, sheaf of wheat (?). Below, Sokaris bark flanked by Anubis jackals. Egypto-Coptic. Late IIIrd-IVth Century. .886 x .43 m.

PROVENANCE: Deir el-Bahari (?).

BIBLIOGRAPHY: *Archaeological Report of the Egypt Exploration Fund*, 1894-95, p. 33, Pl. II.

LENT BY: *The Museum of Fine Arts, Boston.*

For a discussion of this type see Scott-Moncrieff, P. D., *Paganism and Christianity in Egypt*, Cambridge, 1913, pp. 126-130. The Fayum portrait from the collection of Dr. Valentiner should also be compared with Nos. 9 and 10.

*10.   PAINTED CARTONNAGE. Moulded and painted wreath on head, face bearded. Suspended from neck, pectoral (?) with heart scarab. In right hand, a cup; in left, a garland (?). Below, Sokaris bark flanked by Anubis jackals. Coptic. Late IIIrd-early IVth Century. .805 x .32 m.

PROVENANCE: Unknown.

BIBLIOGRAPHY: *Sale Catalogue*, Hood Coll. Sotheby, Nov. 11, 1924, No. 162.

LENT BY: *The Brummer Gallery.*

*11.   TEMPERA PAINTING ON WOOD. Flying angel with gold halo, red and green robes, white wings, exposed portions of body flesh color. Background and details of wings blue (ultra marine). Probably from a tabernacle or ark. Coptic. About VIIth Century. .222 x .192 m.

PROVENANCE: Unknown.

BIBLIOGRAPHY: Unpublished.

LENT BY: *Mr. H. Kevorkian.*

*12.   MINIATURE PAINTING, Madonna and Child. Frontispiece to Synaxary (calendar of saints) written in Coptic (Sahidic dialect). Morgan Ms. 612. Coptic. Dated 893 A. D. .337 x .264 m.

PROVENANCE: Upper Egypt.

BIBLIOGRAPHY: Complete bibliography listed in *Exhibition of Illuminated Manuscripts Held at the New York Public Library*, The Pierpont Morgan Library, 1933, p. 1, No. 1.

LENT BY: *The Pierpont Morgan Library.*

*13.   MINIATURE PAINTING, Madonna and Child. Frontispiece to Liturgy written in Coptic (Sahidic dialect). Morgan Ms. 574. Coptic. Dated 895 or 898 A. D. .279 x .219 m.

PROVENANCE: Upper Egypt.

BIBLIOGRAPHY: Complete bibliography listed in *Exhibition of Illuminated Manuscripts Held at the New York Public Library*, The Pierpont Morgan Library, 1933, p. 1, No. 3.

LENT BY: *The Pierpont Morgan Library.*

*14. MINIATURE PAINTING, Virgin and Saint. Frontispiece to Synaxary written in Coptic (Sahidic dialect). Morgan Ms. 597. Coptic. Dated 914 A. D.   .349 x .251 m.

PROVENANCE: The Fayum.

BIBLIOGRAPHY: Complete bibliography listed in *Exhibition of Illuminated Manuscripts Held at the New York Public Library*, The Pierpont Morgan Library, 1933, p. 5, No. 8.

LENT BY: *The Pierpont Morgan Library.*

15. COPTIC MANUSCRIPT. Gospel of St. Luke on parchment in the Sahidic dialect. 55 folios. VIth Century.

PROVENANCE: Said to be from Magaga.

BIBLIOGRAPHY: Gehman, H. S., *Journal of the American Oriental Society*, Vol. 55, No. 4, pp. 451-457.

LENT BY: *Mr. Robert Garrett.*

STONE SCULPTURE

IN THE ROUND

16. STEATITE STATUETTE OF A PRIESTESS OF ISIS. Originally fitted with headdress. Graeco-Egyptian. Ist Century. .088 m.
PROVENANCE: Unknown. Purchased by W. F. Petrie for the Museum, in Cairo, 1905.
BIBLIOGRAPHY: Unpublished.
Brooklyn Museum Collection.

17. LIMESTONE HEAD OF A QUEEN. Archaistic headdress with uraeus. Egypto-Roman. Probably Ist-IInd Century. .247 m.
PROVENANCE: Unknown.
BIBLIOGRAPHY: Unpublished.
LENT BY: *Walters Art Gallery.*

*18. BLACK BASALT (?) BUST OF A MAN grasping the legs of an animal slung around his shoulders. Eyes originally inlaid. A Hermes (?) statue. Egypto-Roman. Second half of Ist Century. .235 x .24 m. (width at shoulders).
PROVENANCE: "From Lower Egypt".
BIBLIOGRAPHY: Unpublished.
Abbott Collection. From the Collections of the New York Historical Society in the Brooklyn Museum.

19. BLACK BASALT MALE PORTRAIT HEAD. Eyes originally inlaid. Conventionalized curly hair. Egypto-Roman. IInd Century, or later. .12 m.
PROVENANCE: Unknown.
BIBLIOGRAPHY: Ex. coll. Henry Wallis, *Sale Catalogue,* Sotheby, June 9, 1937, No. 46. Cf. Strzygowski, *Koptische Kunst,* p. 16, Abb. 16.
LENT BY: *The Brummer Gallery.*

*20. BLACK BASALT MALE HEAD. Stone left uncut behind the ears. Head made separately for attachment to body. Egypto-Roman. Late Ist-early IInd Century. .305 m.
PROVENANCE: Unknown.
BIBLIOGRAPHY: Unpublished.
LENT BY: *The Brummer Gallery.*

21. GRAY GRANITE ANIMAL HEAD. Perhaps a panther, snarling. Long neck with encircling cord near base. Detail from a larger composition. Graeco-Egyptian. Period uncertain, possibly IInd-IIIrd Century .44 m.
PROVENANCE: Alexandria.
BIBLIOGRAPHY: Unpublished. Cf. Strzygowski, *Koptische Kunst*, p. 15, Abb. 13.
LENT BY: *The Brummer Gallery*.

22. POLISHED BRECCIA URN. Pink and black veining. One handle missing. Egypto-Roman. Probably Ist-IInd Century. .292 x .26 m. (diameter at rim).
PROVENANCE: Alexandria.
BIBLIOGRAPHY: Unpublished.
LENT BY: *The Brummer Gallery*.

23. YELLOW ONYX SERAPIS (?) HEAD. Flat modelling on face. Head apparently made as a separate piece. Graeco-Egyptian (probably Alexandrian work). IInd (?) Century. .119 m.
PROVENANCE: Unknown.
BIBLIOGRAPHY: Unpublished.
LENT BY: *The Brummer Gallery*.

*24. BLACK GRANITE MALE PORTRAIT HEAD. Face bearded. Remains of plinth at base of neck. Egypto-Roman. Probably IIIrd Century. .16 m.
PROVENANCE: Unknown.
BIBLIOGRAPHY: Ex. coll. Henry Wallis, *Sale Catalogue*, Sotheby, June 9, 1937, No. 46.
LENT BY: *The Brummer Gallery*.

*25. BLACK GRANITE HEAD OF A MAN. Egypto-Roman. Late IIIrd Century. .118 m.
PROVENANCE: Unknown.
BIBLIOGRAPHY: Unpublished.
LENT BY: *Walters Art Gallery*.

26. GREEN BASALT SERAPIS (?) HEAD. Modelling of face and back of head very shallow. Drill holes throughout beard and hair (in front). Stylized hair on back of head. Graeco-Egyptian. Based on work of the IInd Century B. C. but probably IIIrd-IVth (?) Century A. D. .12 m
PROVENANCE: Unknown.

BIBLIOGRAPHY: Unpublished.
LENT BY: *The Brummer Gallery.*

27. LIMESTONE HEAD OF A WOMAN. Stylized hair. Large earrings of late Hellenistic type. Coptic. IIIrd-IVth (?) Century. .21 m.
PROVENANCE: Unknown.
BIBLIOGRAPHY: *Important Documents of Coptic Art*, D. G. Kelekian, New York, [1929].
LENT BY: *Mr. Dikran G. Kelekian.*

*28. HAEMATITE HEAD OF A WOMAN. Egypto-Coptic. IIIrd-Vth (?) Century. .07 m.
PROVENANCE: Unknown.
BIBLIOGRAPHY: Unpublished.
LENT BY: *The Brummer Gallery.*

*29. LIMESTONE MALE HEAD. Conventionalized hair and beard retaining extensive traces of black paint. Remains of red paint on lips. Head made separately with long cylindrical boring at base of neck for attachment to body. Coptic. IVth-Vth Century. .115 m.
PROVENANCE: Said to be from Bawit.
BIBLIOGRAPHY: Unpublished.
LENT BY: *Mr. H. Kevorkian.*

*30. LIMESTONE LION. Probably a support for a pilaster. The sculpture was probably one of a pair flanking a door. Head in the round, body in high relief. Around the neck, floral wreath of the type found on faience jars. Coptic. Vth-VIth Century. .286 x .483 m.
PROVENANCE: Unknown.
BIBLIOGRAPHY: *Important Documents of Coptic Art*, D. G. Kelekian, New York, [1929].
LENT BY: *Mr. Dikran G. Kelekian.*

31. BLACK BASALT BIRD. Probably a detail from a larger composition. Coptic. Probably Vth-VIth Century. .038 x .06 m.
PROVENANCE: Unknown.
BIBLIOGRAPHY: Unpublished.
LENT BY: *Dumbarton Oaks Collection.*

*32. IRONSTONE STATUETTE. Probably representing an Apostle. Coptic. VIth-VIIth Century. .142 m.

PROVENANCE: Akhmim.

BIBLIOGRAPHY: Unpublished.

LENT BY: *Walters Art Gallery.*

STELAE

*33. LIMESTONE FUNERARY STELA of C. Julius Valerius standing in an aedicula. With his right hand he pours incense (?) on an altar; in his left, a situla. To the right, a griffin. On brackets, at left, an Anubis jackal (?); at right, a Horus falcon. Below, four lines of Latin giving his name, genealogy and age (three) at death. Egyptian. IIIrd (?) Century. .357 x .258 m.

PROVENANCE: Unknown. Purchased by Charles Edwin Wilbour in Cairo, November 6, 1881.

BIBLIOGRAPHY: Wilbour, C. E., *Travels in Egypt*, Brooklyn Museum, 1936, illustrated on Pl. opposite p. 88 and briefly mentioned, p. 74.

Wilbour Collection, Brooklyn Museum.

A similar example is in Bissing, *Denkmäler agyptischer Sculptur*, Munich, 1914, Vol. II, Pl. 121.

*34. LIMESTONE STELA. Reclining man and woman on couch. At right, an orans. Couch flanked by Anubis jackals. Below, two lines of Greek. Remains of red paint. Coptic. IIIrd-IVth Century. .35 x .402 m.

PROVENANCE: Said to be from Akhmim.

BIBLIOGRAPHY: Unpublished.

LENT BY: *Walters Art Gallery.*

*35. LIMESTONE FUNERARY STELA of Chairemon, orans, standing in an aedicula and flanked by Anubis jackals. Inscribed at base in two lines of Greek. Coptic. IVth-Vth (?) Century. .389 x .335 m.

PROVENANCE: Kom el-Ahmar.

BIBLIOGRAPHY: Unpublished.

Wilbour Collection, Brooklyn Museum.

Numerous stelae of this type are known but the dating is uncertain. Some have Coptic inscriptions, thus making the IVth Century the earliest probable date.

*36. LIMESTONE FUNERARY STELA with nude male figure standing in an aedicula. Laurel wreath on head, right hand grasps laurel branch. Ankh sign above right column. Gable inscribed in Greek: "Olympios, age twenty-seven". Coptic. Vth Century. .378 x .29 m.
PROVENANCE: Unknown.
BIBLIOGRAPHY: Exhibited at the Worcester Art Museum, *The Dark Ages*, Worcester, 1937, No. 43. Otherwise unpublished.
Brooklyn Museum Collection.
   The figure probably represents Olympios as a beatified deceased and is undoubtedly intended as an orans, the right arm being lowered to make room for the laurel branch.

37. LIMESTONE STELA. Phoebammon, orans, within columns. Coptic. VIth-VIIth Century. .93 x .435 m.
PROVENANCE: From the Fayum (?).
BIBLIOGRAPHY: *Handbook of the Egyptian Rooms*, Metropolitan Museum, 1911, p. 158.
LENT BY: *Metropolitan Museum of Art.*

*38. SANDSTONE STELA. In center, pelican (?) flanked by columns. Floral and geometric decorations. Below, Coptic inscription. Coptic. VIIth-VIIIth Century. .36 x .257 m.
PROVENANCE: Esneh.
BIBLIOGRAPHY: Unpublished.
LENT BY: *The Museum of Fine Arts, Boston.*

*39. SANDSTONE STELA. Eagle within an aedicula flanked by peacocks and deer. Below, two crosses within arches. Coptic. VIIth-VIIIth Century. .585 x .43 m.
PROVENANCE: Esneh.
BIBLIOGRAPHY: Unpublished.
LENT BY: *The Museum of Fine Arts, Boston.*

RELIEFS AND ARCHITECTURAL FRAGMENTS

*40. FRAGMENT OF LIMESTONE FRIEZE. Alternating boars and lambs within conventionalized grapevine. Coptic. Probably Vth Century. .355 x 1.28 m.
PROVENANCE: Unknown.
BIBLIOGRAPHY: Unpublished.

LENT BY: *The University Museum, Philadelphia.*

A well known type found at least as early as the IVth Century. A very similar though less complete example is in the Walters Art Gallery, Baltimore, (*Handbook,* 1936, p. 53).

*41.   COMPACT LIMESTONE FRIEZE. Conventionalized grapevine enclosing baskets of fruit and birds. Coptic. Vth Century. .18 x 1.03 m.
PROVENANCE: Said to be from Bawit.
BIBLIOGRAPHY: Unpublished. A very similar frieze from the south end of Chapel X at Bawit is in the Louvre.
LENT BY: *Mr. H. Kevorkian.*

*42.   LIMESTONE RELIEF. Grapevine forming crosses within circles. Hare and lion between circles facing in opposite directions. White paint on background, red paint on relief. Coptic. Vth-VIth Century. .332 x .477 m.
PROVENANCE: Unknown.
BIBLIOGRAPHY: Unpublished.
LENT BY: *Pratt Institute.*

43.   LIMESTONE RELIEF. Lion attacking gazelle amidst grapevine. Coptic. Vth Century. .345 x .725 m.
PROVENANCE: Unknown.
BIBLIOGRAPHY: *Important Documents of Coptic Art,* D. G. Kelekian, New York, [1929].
LENT BY: *Mr. Dikran G. Kelekian.*

*44.   LIMESTONE CAPITAL. Oblong with flaring top. Acanthus decoration. At base, a crouching ram. Coptic. Vth Century. .42 x .85 x .42 m.
PROVENANCE: Said to be from Bawit.
BIBLIOGRAPHY: Unpublished. For a similar specimen see Simaika, M. H., *Guide sommaire du Musée copte,* Cairo, 1937, No. 4325, p. 12, Pl. XXIV.
LENT BY: *Mr. H. Kevorkian.*

*45.   FOUR ENGAGED LIMESTONE ARCHES. Engaged pilasters with conventionalized vine motifs of varying type. Arches decorated with combined late Hellenistic architectural motifs. Crossbars (stone) decorated with conventionalized laurel bands. At base of arches, conventionalized grapevine reliefs. Coptic. Late Vth Century. 3.20 x 2.45 m. (single arch).

PROVENANCE: Said to be from Bawit.

BIBLIOGRAPHY: Unpublished.

LENT BY: *Mr. H. Kevorkian.*

    Detail only illustrated.

46.   LIMESTONE RELIEF. A dove and a peacock between large conventionalized flowers. Coptic. Late Vth-VIth Century. .145 x .367 m.

PROVENANCE: Said to be from Bawit.

BIBLIOGRAPHY: Unpublished.

LENT BY: *Mr. H. Kevorkian.*

47.   SECTION OF A LIMESTONE COLUMN. Vertical registers of deeply cut acanthus leaves. Coptic. Vth-VIth Century. .725 x .305 m. (diameter).

PROVENANCE: Unknown.

BIBLIOGRAPHY: *Important Documents of Coptic Art,* D. G. Kelekian, New York, [1929].

LENT BY: *Mr. Dikran G. Kelekian.*

*48.   LIMESTONE WATER-JAR STAND. Probably a re-used architectural fragment. Front decorated with reliefs of vines and fish. Drainage hole in center masked with female head. Interior has circular jar support at each end draining into central oblong depression. Coptic. Vth-VIth Century. .275 x .85 x .29 m.

PROVENANCE: Unknown.

BIBLIOGRAPHY: Unpublished.

LENT BY: *Mr. Dikran G. Kelekian.*

*49.   ENGAGED LIMESTONE CAPITAL. In center, monogrammed cross flanked by peacocks. Below, acanthus motifs; above, grapevine. Coptic. Vth-VIth Century. .48 x .81 x .175 m.

PROVENANCE: Said to be from Bawit.

BIBLIOGRAPHY: Unpublished. For another example of this monogrammed cross see Dalton, O. M., *Byzantine Art and Archaeology,* Oxford, 1911, p. 95, Fig. 55, silver dish of the VIth Century.

LENT BY: *Mr. H. Kevorkian.*

*50. **ENGAGED LIMESTONE CAPITAL.** Companion piece to the preceding example. Variations in monogram and central design of cross. Coptic. Vth-VIth Century. .48 x .81 x .175 m.
PROVENANCE: Said to be from Bawit.
BIBLIOGRAPHY: Unpublished.
LENT BY: *Mr. H. Kevorkian.*

51. **LIMESTONE RELIEF.** Genius, probably one of a pair, supporting a medallion. Grapevine design on balance. Coptic. Vth-VIth Century. .22 x .555 m.
PROVENANCE: Unknown.
BIBLIOGRAPHY: Unpublished.
LENT BY: *Mr. Dikran G. Kelekian.*

*52. **LIMESTONE FRIEZE.** Conventionalized grapevine forming scrolls. Within each scroll, a bunch of grapes. Coptic. Vth-VIth Century. .31 x 1.50 m.
PROVENANCE: Said to be from Bawit.
BIBLIOGRAPHY: Unpublished.
LENT BY: *Mr. H. Kevorkian.*

*53. **LIMESTONE FRIEZE.** Laurel bands forming medallions containing alternating representations of portrait heads and conventionalized flowers. Coptic. Vth-VIth Century. .325 x 1.43 m.
PROVENANCE: Said to be from Bawit.
BIBLIOGRAPHY: Unpublished.
LENT BY: *Mr. H. Kevorkian.*

54. **LIMESTONE RELIEF.** At each end, a lion (?) in front of a palm tree. Between the lions, a ram. Above, human head with cross. Possibly a conventionalized representation of the martyrdom of St. Thekla. Coptic. Late Vth-early VIth Century. .26 x .655 m.
PROVENANCE: Unknown.
BIBLIOGRAPHY: *Important Documents of Coptic Art,* D. G. Kelekian, New York, [1929].
LENT BY: *Mr. Dikran G. Kelekian.*

55. **LIMESTONE RELIEF.** In center, urn flanked by peacocks. Details of bodies painted. At right end, a grapevine. Coptic. Vth-VIth Century. .415 x .825 m.

26

PROVENANCE: Unknown.
BIBLIOGRAPHY: Unpublished.
LENT BY: *Mr. Dikran G. Kelekian.*

56. LIMESTONE FRIEZE. Conventionalized grapevine forming scrolls. At left end, a fish. Coptic. Vth-VIth Century. .30 x .895 m.
PROVENANCE: Said to be from Bawit.
BIBLIOGRAPHY: Unpublished.
LENT BY: *Mr. H. Kevorkian.*

*57. LIMESTONE GABLE. In center, large urn flanked by pair of gambolling deer. Conventionalized grapevine on remainder of surface. Coptic. About VIth Century. .278 x .87 m.
PROVENANCE: Unknown.
BIBLIOGRAPHY: *Important Documents of Coptic Art,* D. G. Kelekian, New York, [1929].
LENT BY: *Mr. Dikran G. Kelekian.*

*58. LIMESTONE RELIEF. Probably St. Sisinnios mounted on horseback piercing his sister with a lance. Coptic. About VIth Century. .383 x .58 m.
PROVENANCE: Unknown. Doubtless a companion piece to the following relief.
BIBLIOGRAPHY: Unpublished. For a similar composition in painting see, de Gruneisen, W., *Les caractéristiques de l'art copte,* Florence, 1922, Pl. XXXV, No. 1, pp. 63-64. For the story of St. Sisinnios see O'Leary, De Lacy, *The Saints of Egypt,* London, 1937, pp. 258-9.
Brooklyn Museum Collection.

Probably from the same site as the following relief. Each relief shows strong Syrian influence and it is not impossible that they are of Syrian rather than Egyptian origin. The subject is fairly common in Coptic art but is variously interpreted. The frequent description as that of a military saint is too comprehensive and uncertain. Strzygowski believes it a representation of the triumph of good over evil based on the Mazdean religion. Terra cotta figures of Graeco-Egyptian gods dating from the earliest centuries of our era are also found seated on animals but their meaning is unknown.

*59. LIMESTONE RELIEF. Probably portraying the martyrdom of St. Thekla who was torn to pieces by lions. Conventionalized foliate background. Coptic. About VIth Century. .335 x .583 m.
PROVENANCE: Unknown.

BIBLIOGRAPHY: Exhibited at Worcester Art Museum, *The Dark Ages*, Worcester,
1937, Pl. 49. Otherwise unpublished.
Brooklyn Museum Collection.

*60. LIMESTONE RELIEF. Lion attacking gazelle. Conventionalized
grapevine fills background. Coptic. About VIth Century. .205 x .53 m.
PROVENANCE: Unknown.
BIBLIOGRAPHY: Unpublished.
Brooklyn Museum Collection.

A common subject in Coptic reliefs and textiles. It probably has no
iconographic significance.

61. PAIR OF ENGAGED LIMESTONE COLUMNS with separate capitals.
Sides of columns flat and decorated with conventionalized vine motifs.
Two registers of conventionalized vine details across front of each column.
On front face of each capital, a fantastic animal, above which and on
sides, are conventionalized vine details. Traces of blue and red paint
on grapevine. Animals originally painted blue. Coptic. Probably
VIth Century. .80 m.
PROVENANCE: Said to be from Bawit.
BIBLIOGRAPHY: Unpublished.
LENT BY: *Mr. H. Kevorkian.*

62. ARCHITECTURAL DETAIL. Acanthus decoration with female head
in center. Limestone. Coptic. VIth Century. .255 x .50 m.
PROVENANCE: Said to be from Bawit.
BIBLIOGRAPHY: Unpublished.
LENT BY: *Mr. H. Kevorkian.*

63. RELIEF FRAGMENT. In high relief, a lion facing backwards. Limestone. Coptic. VIth Century. .255 x .435 m.
PROVENANCE: Unknown.
BIBLIOGRAPHY: Unpublished.
LENT BY: *Mr. Dikran G. Kelekian.*

*64. FRAGMENTARY WOODEN PANEL. Conventionalized vine design and laurel band forming ovoid medallions. In central medallion, incomplete mythological scene. Coptic. Probably Vth Century. .215 x 1.49 m.

PROVENANCE: Said to be from Bawit.

BIBLIOGRAPHY: Unpublished.

LENT BY: *Mr. H. Kevorkian.*

*65. WOODEN PANEL. Interlacing medallions enclosing conventionalized flowers. The design is common in textiles of the period. Coptic. Probably Vth Century. .223 x 1.48 m.

PROVENANCE: Said to be from Bawit.

BIBLIOGRAPHY: Unpublished.

LENT BY: *Mr. H. Kevorkian.*

*66. WOODEN PANEL. In center, portrait medallion flanked by laurel festoons enclosing Nilotic scenes. At ends, conventionalized flowers within medallions. Coptic. Probably Vth Century. .238 x 1.30 m.

PROVENANCE: Said to be from Bawit.

BIBLIOGRAPHY: Unpublished.

LENT BY: *Mr. H. Kevorkian.*

*67. WOODEN PANEL. Conventionalized vine forming medallions enclosing busts of a nimbed orans alternating with pelicans. Traces of red and black paint on background. Such panels were frequently set in place between capitals under an arch in churches. Coptic. Probably Vth Century. .245 x 1.52 m.

PROVENANCE: Unknown.

BIBLIOGRAPHY: *Important Documents of Coptic Art,* D. G. Kelekian, New York, [1929].

LENT BY: *Mr. Dikran G. Kelekian.*
Detail only illustrated.

68. WOODEN PANEL. Central medallion with flanking animals. Balance of field filled with floral and geometric designs. At each end, a large eagle. Coptic. About VIIth Century. .253 x 1.32 m.

PROVENANCE: Unknown.

BIBLIOGRAPHY: Unpublished.

LENT BY: *Mr. Dikran G. Kelekian.*

69. **WOODEN PANEL.** Wild animals fighting. Foliage background. Coptic. VIth Century. .11 x .215 m.
PROVENANCE: Unknown.
BIBLIOGRAPHY: Unpublished.
LENT BY: *Mr. Dikran G. Kelekian.*

*70. **WOODEN FIGURE OF A SAINT** clasping book in left hand. Right arm raised in blessing. Probably an inlay. Coptic. Period uncertain. .218 x .085 m.
PROVENANCE: Unknown.
BIBLIOGRAPHY: Unpublished.
Brooklyn Museum Collection.

*71. **SMALL WOODEN DOOR** opening from the left. In raised relief, a saint, orans. To the left, an iron lock requiring five turns of a key to open. Extensive remains of paint. Probably from a small chest or tabernacle. Coptic. VIIth (?) Century. .161 x .148 m.
PROVENANCE: Unknown.
BIBLIOGRAPHY: Unpublished.
Brooklyn Museum Collection.

72. **SMALL WOODEN PANEL** with standing angel grasping staff ending in small cross. Wings extend to ground. The details of the face were painted. Coptic. Period uncertain. .167 x .106 m.
PROVENANCE: Unknown.
BIBLIOGRAPHY: Unpublished.
Brooklyn Museum Collection.

*73. **WOODEN COMB.** On central panel openwork design of peacock within foliage. Coptic. About VIth Century. .21 x .08 m.
PROVENANCE: Akhmim.
BIBLIOGRAPHY: Unpublished.
LENT BY: *The Museum of Fine Arts, Boston.*

74. **WOODEN COMB.** Sides and central panel decorated with concentric circles. Coptic. About VIth-VIIth Century. .093 m. (length).
PROVENANCE: Unknown.
BIBLIOGRAPHY: Unpublished.
LENT BY: *The Museum of Fine Arts, Boston.*

75. WOODEN COMB. Central panel decorated on obverse with geometric design of incised circles. Coptic. About Vth-VIIth Century. .229 x .072 m.

PROVENANCE: Unknown.
BIBLIOGRAPHY: Unpublished.
LENT BY: *Johns Hopkins University Archaeological Museum.*

76. WEAVER'S WOODEN COMB. Decorated on observe and reverse with geometric designs. Coptic. VIth-VIIth Century. .243 x .085 m.

PROVENANCE: Unknown.
BIBLIOGRAPHY: Unpublished.
LENT BY: *Johns Hopkins University Archaeological Museum.*

77. WEAVER'S WOODEN COMB. Decorated on obverse and reverse with concentric circles. Coptic. VIth-VIIth Century. .22 x .08 m.

PROVENANCE: Unknown.
BIBLIOGRAPHY: Unpublished.
LENT BY: *Johns Hopkins University Archaeological Museum.*

*78. WOODEN PANEL, probably from an altar screen. Sacrifice of Isaac. Elaborate foliate background. Extensive remains of gold leaf on gesso base. Coptic. Xth-XIth Century. .199 x .137 m.

PROVENANCE: Said to be from the church of Abu Sarga, Old Cairo.
BIBLIOGRAPHY: Unpublished.
LENT BY: *Mr. H. Kevorkian.*

BRONZE

79. **BRONZE BOWL.** On interior, at center, incised lotus flower; next, incised grapevine, then a chevron band. Probably treated as niello work. Coptic. IInd-IVth Century. .064 x .179 m.

PROVENANCE: Unknown.
BIBLIOGRAPHY: Unpublished.
LENT BY: *Professor Vladimir G. Simkhovitch.*

A transitional design. Compare the similar piece in Strzygowski, *Koptische Kunst,* p. 271, No. 9073.

*80. **BRONZE STATUETTE.** Hercules (?) running. Fillet around the head with ends resting on shoulders. Schematized face and body. Cast solid. Roman. Second half of IIIrd Century. .312 m.

PROVENANCE: Said to be from Alexandria.
BIBLIOGRAPHY: Unpublished.
Brooklyn Museum Collection.

*81. **BRONZE CUP.** On lower part of body, silver inlay of half-lozenges interspersed with crosses; above, Coptic inscription inlaid in silver. Coptic. IVth-VIth Century. .102 x .133 m.

PROVENANCE: Said to be from the Fayum.
BIBLIOGRAPHY: Unpublished.
LENT BY: *Mr. Robert Garrett.*

*82. **BRONZE VESSEL.** On lower part of body, Coptic inscription inlaid in silver; above, silver inlays of crosses. Coptic. IVth-VIth Century. .14 x .215 m.

PROVENANCE: Said to be from the Fayum.
BIBLIOGRAPHY: Unpublished.
LENT BY: *Mr. Robert Garrett.*

A similar undecorated specimen is in Strzygowski, *Koptische Kunst,* Pl. XXVIII, No. 9066.

*83. **BRONZE LAMP.** Handle, a cross within circle surmounted by dove. Coptic. IVth-VIth Century. .075 x .086 m.

PROVENANCE: Unknown. Purchased at Luxor, Egypt, in March, 1889, by Charles Edwin Wilbour.
BIBLIOGRAPHY: Unpublished.
Wilbour Collection, Brooklyn Museum.

84. BRONZE CROSS. Corners of each arm rounded. Coptic inscription (probably a monogram) of three letters inscribed on central part. Small bronze dowel for attachment at base. Coptic. About Vth Century. .166 x .119 m.

PROVENANCE: Unknown.

BIBLIOGRAPHY: Unpublished. Cf. Strzygowski, *Koptische Kunst*, Pl. XXXV, No. 9177; Pl. XXXIX, No. 7201.

LENT BY: *The Brummer Gallery.*

*85. BRONZE INCENSE BURNER (or possibly a lamp holder). Tripod base with claw feet supporting baluster surmounted by bowl. On rim, series of openwork rings each surmounted by a conventionalized dove. On exterior of bowl, in punch-work, three lines of Greek. Coptic. About Vth Century. .285 x .138 m. (diam. of bowl).

PROVENANCE: Unknown.

BIBLIOGRAPHY: *Exposition internationale d'art byzantine*, Paris, 1931, No. 413.

LENT BY: *The Brummer Gallery.*

*86. BRONZE POLYCANDELON. Cross within a circle. Openings on cross and rim for insertion of lamps. Three suspension rings. Coptic. Vth-VIth Century. .577 m.

PROVENANCE: Said to be from Bawit.

BIBLIOGRAPHY: Unpublished. A duplicate companion piece is in the Louvre.

LENT BY: *Mr. H. Kevorkian.*

*87. BRONZE INCENSE BURNER. Square body decorated with incised concentric circles. Pyramidal cover with openwork designs; on back and front, crosses flanked by lions rampant and, on sides, naturalistic grapevine. Cross surmounts cover. Coptic. Vth (?) Century. .191 x .072 m.

PROVENANCE: Unknown.

BIBLIOGRAPHY: Unpublished.

LENT BY: *Dumbarton Oaks Collection.*

88. BRONZE LAMP ON PRICKET STAND. Small cross soldered to body of lamp. Coptic. Vth-VIth Century. .356 m.

PROVENANCE: Unknown.

BIBLIOGRAPHY: Unpublished.

LENT BY: *Mr. H. Kevorkian.*

*89. **BRONZE LAMP ON PRICKET STAND.** Conch cover on lamp. Handle in form of cross. Coptic. About VIth Century. .323 m.
PROVENANCE: Unknown.
BIBLIOGRAPHY: Unpublished.
LENT BY: *Mr. H. Kevorkian.*

*90. **BRONZE PROCESSIONAL CROSS** on bronze standard. Probably to be fitted to a wooden staff. Coptic. About VIth Century. .425 x .215 m.
PROVENANCE: Unknown.
BIBLIOGRAPHY: Kaufmann, Das koptische Tubenkreuz, in *Oriens Christianus*, N. S., Vol. IV, 1915, pp. 306-11.
LENT BY: *Metropolitan Museum of Art.*

*91. **BRONZE CENSER.** In relief, scenes of the Annunciation, Nativity, Baptism, Crucifixion and Holy Women at the Sepulcher. Coptic. About VIth-VIIth Century. .13 x .108 m.
PROVENANCE: Unknown.
BIBLIOGRAPHY: Exhibited at the Worcester Art Museum, *The Dark Ages*, Worcester, 1937, No. 113.
LENT BY: *The Brummer Gallery.*

92. **BRONZE CENSER.** In relief, scenes of the Baptism, Crucifixion, Holy Women at Sepulcher, Annunciation and Nativity. Coptic. About VIth-VIIth Century. .084 x .073 m.
PROVENANCE: Unknown.
BIBLIOGRAPHY: Unpublished.
LENT BY: *Mr. H. Kevorkian.*

*93. **BRONZE LAMP** in the form of a peacock. Incised circles on body. Coptic. About VIth-VIIth Century. .154 x .13 m.
PROVENANCE: Unknown.
BIBLIOGRAPHY: Unpublished.
LENT BY: *Dumbarton Oaks Collection.*

94. **BRONZE LITURGICAL EWER.** Perforated cover. Standing lion on handle. Coptic. About VIIIth (?) Century. .249 m.
PROVENANCE: Unknown.
BIBLIOGRAPHY: Unpublished. A similar, undated specimen is in the British Museum.
LENT BY: *Mr. H. Kevorkian.*

*95. BONE CARVING. Nilotic scene. Alexandrian type. Probably IIIrd-Vth Century. .052 x .112 m.
PROVENANCE: Unknown.
BIBLIOGRAPHY: Unpublished.
LENT BY: *Mr. and Mrs. William R. Tyler.*

*96. BONE PLAQUE. Dancing woman clasping in right hand a bunch of grapes. Alexandrian type. IIIrd-Vth Century. .095 x .04 m.
PROVENANCE: Unknown.
BIBLIOGRAPHY: Unpublished.
LENT BY: *Johns Hopkins University Archaeological Museum.*

*97. WOODEN BOX with carved and painted bone panels depicting figures of Alexandrian type. Extensive portions of wooden mounting probably modern. Coptic. About IVth-Vth Century. .35 x .33 x .298 m.
PROVENANCE: Unknown.
BIBLIOGRAPHY: *Exposition d'art byzantine,* Paris, 1931, No. 12. Ross, M. C., "Coptic Art Survey in a New Gallery", in *The Art News,* March 4, 1939, p. 10.
LENT BY: *Walters Art Gallery.*

*98. WOOD AND IVORY BOX. Ivory decorated with incised concentric circles. Probably Coptic. IVth-VIIth Century. .095 x .17 x .12 m.
PROVENANCE: Akhmim.
BIBLIOGRAPHY: Unpublished.
LENT BY: *The Museum of Fine Arts, Boston.*

*99. IVORY PANEL. In relief, undulating grapevine. Coptic. Late IVth-early Vth Century. .04 x .124 m.
PROVENANCE: Sakkara.
BIBLIOGRAPHY: Unpublished.
Abbott Collection. From the Collections of the New York Historical Society in the Brooklyn Museum.

*100. IVORY COMB. On central panel, obverse, foliate pattern; reverse, flanking peacocks (?). Coptic. About Vth-VIth Century. .088 x .055 m.

PROVENANCE: Unknown. Purchased by Charles Edwin Wilbour at Abydos, March, 1887.

BIBLIOGRAPHY: Unpublished.

Wilbour Collection, Brooklyn Museum.

*101.   FRAGMENT OF IVORY RELIEF. Probably Venus or Daphne. Surface stained brown. Coptic. Vth Century. .11 m.

PROVENANCE: Unknown.

BIBLIOGRAPHY: Unpublished. Compare with relief at Ravenna representing Daphne turning into tree.

LENT BY: *Walters Art Gallery.*

102.   FOUR CONVEX BONE CARVINGS. Conventional floral and vine motifs. Pierced. All four pieces probably from the same object. Coptic. Vth-VIth Century.

PROVENANCE: Said to be from Alexandria.

BIBLIOGRAPHY: Unpublished.

Brooklyn Museum Collection.

*103.   BONE TUSK. On front surface, grapevine interspersed with animals and vessels. Traces of red and green paint. Coptic. Vth-VIth Century. .023 x .108 m.

PROVENANCE: Unknown.

BIBLIOGRAPHY: Unpublished.

LENT BY: *Johns Hopkins University Archaeological Museum.*

*104.   IVORY PYXIS. In relief, Discord with the Apple at the Banquet and the Judgment of Paris. Probably Alexandrian work. Coptic. About 500 A. D. .085 x .09 m. (diameter).

PROVENANCE: Unknown.

BIBLIOGRAPHY: Ex. coll. Possenti (sale, Florence, March 29, 1880, No. 16, Pl. 15).

LENT BY: *Walters Art Gallery.*

*105.   PAINTED IVORY PYXIS. The reliefs represent Moses receiving the Law and Daniel in the Lions' Den. Probably of Alexandrian workmanship. Coptic. Early VIth Century. .092 x .102 m.

PROVENANCE: Unknown. Formerly in the Abbey Church of Moggio.

BIBLIOGRAPHY: Venturi, L., in *L'Arte,* 1911, p. 469 ff. Exhibited at Worcester Art Museum, *The Dark Ages,* Worcester, 1936, No. 57. Morey, C. R., *Art News,* Feb. 30, 1937, p. 15.

LENT BY: *Dumbarton Oaks Collection.*

*106.   **BONE INLAY PANEL.** Female figure, frontal, probably Aphrodite. Coptic. VIth-VIIth Century. .08 m.
PROVENANCE: Unknown.
BIBLIOGRAPHY: Ex. coll. Duke Alexander Michaelovitch.
LENT BY: *Walters Art Gallery.*

*107.   **IVORY INLAY.** In relief, Sasanid king, frontal, seated within an arch. Sword grasped in both hands. Coptic. VIIth Century. .176 x .098 m.
PROVENANCE: Unknown.
BIBLIOGRAPHY: Unpublished. Cf. paper read at the meeting of the American Oriental Society, March, 1940, Ross, M. C., "A Coptic Bone Carving in the Walters Art Gallery". To be published in *Bulletin de la Société des amis de l'art copte*, Cairo.
LENT BY: *Walters Art Gallery.*

*108.   **CONVEX IVORY RELIEF.** The Virgin, frontal, holding the Child against her cheek. At sides, above, flanking angels. Surface stained brown. Coptic. IXth-Xth Century. .262 m.
PROVENANCE: Unknown.
BIBLIOGRAPHY: Exhibited at the Worcester Art Museum, *The Dark Ages*, Worcester, 1937, No. 61; Pub. Dr. Aus'm Weerths, *Fundgruben und Ikonographie in dem Elfenbein-Arbeiten*, Bonn, 1912, Pl. 16; A. Goldschmidt in *Parnassus*, March, 1937. Ex. colls. P. Leven (1853), Meyers (1877), Garthe (1877), Hirsch auf Gereuth (1878), M. Boy (Paris, May, 1905, No. 240).
LENT BY: *Walters Art Gallery.*

109. **BLUE GLASS HEAD OF SERAPIS.** Egypto-Roman. Based on a work of the IInd Century B. C., but probably Ist-IInd Century A. D. Egyptian. .079 m.
     PROVENANCE: Unknown.
     BIBLIOGRAPHY: Unpublished. Cf. Froehner, *Cat. Coll. Julian Greau*, 1903, p. 46, No. 271, Pl. XXXII, 1 and 2.
     LENT BY: *Walters Art Gallery.*

110. **CYLINDRICAL FAIENCE JAR.** Pale blue glaze. In high relief, conventionalized hunting scene. Egyptian (probably Alexandrian work). Early (?) Roman period. .107 x .12 m.
     PROVENANCE: Unknown.
     BIBLIOGRAPHY: Ex. coll. MacGregor, *Sale Catalogue*, Sotheby, 1922, No. 322.
     LENT BY: *Walters Art Gallery.*

111. **FAIENCE JAR.** Light green glaze. In relief, centaur and lion separated by stylized floral motifs. Egyptian (probably Alexandrian work). Roman period. .13 x .121 m.
     PROVENANCE: Unknown.
     BIBLIOGRAPHY: Ex. coll. Dattari, *Sale Catalogue*, 1922, No. 322. Cf. De Grüneisen, W., *Les caractéristiques de l'art copte*, p. 9, Figs. 4, 5, note 2.
     LENT BY: *Walters Art Gallery.*

112. **FAIENCE JAR WITH COVER.** Dark blue glaze on body. In high relief, vine decorations in light green glaze. Coptic. IIIrd-IVth Century. .173 m.
     PROVENANCE: Unknown.
     BIBLIOGRAPHY: Unpublished.
     LENT BY: *Mr. Dikran G. Kelekian.*

113. **PAINTED POTTERY JAR.** Buff body. On upper part of body, naturalistic grapevine in purple and black and, above, three crocodiles and stylized bird. Meroitic. After Christ, perhaps IIIrd-IVth (?) Century. .205 x .227 m.
     PROVENANCE: Kerma, Tomb K 18, No. 2.
     BIBLIOGRAPHY: Reisner, G. A., Excavations at Kerma, *Harvard African Studies*, Vol. 5, p. 44, Figs. 15, 36.
     LENT BY: *The Museum of Fine Arts, Boston.*

The undoubted connections between Meroitic, Nubian and Coptic pottery designs have been little studied. Comprehensive groups of excavated specimens are available in the Museum of Fine Arts, Boston, and in the University Museum, Philadelphia.

114. FAIENCE VASE, globular body, cylindrical neck, frieze of fantastic animals around body. Traces of blue glaze on background. Frieze in brown glaze with black details. Coptic. IVth-Vth Century (?) .175 m.
PROVENANCE: Unknown.
BIBLIOGRAPHY: Unpublished.
LENT BY: *Mr. Dikran G. Kelekian.*

115. BLUE FAIENCE VASE. Frieze of animals and birds around body and neck. Coptic. IVth-Vth (?) Century. .154 m.
PROVENANCE: Unknown.
BIBLIOGRAPHY: Unpublished.
LENT BY: *Walters Art Gallery.*

116. BLUE FAIENCE HEAD. Laurel crown. Coptic. About IVth (?) Century. .143 m.
PROVENANCE: Unknown.
BIBLIOGRAPHY: Ex. coll. Dattari, *Sale Catalogue,* 1912, No. 492.
LENT BY: *Walters Art Gallery.*

*117. BLUE FAIENCE FEMALE HEAD. Coptic. IVth-Vth (?) Century. .094 m.
PROVENANCE: Unknown.
BIBLIOGRAPHY: Ex. Coll. Dattari, *Sale Catalogue,* 1912, No. 490.
LENT BY: *Walters Art Gallery.*

118. FAIENCE VASE. Handles joining wide rim to body. Incised grape-vine motif on body. Blue-green glaze. Coptic. About Vth Century. .164 m.
PROVENANCE: Said to be from the Fayum.
BIBLIOGRAPHY: Wallis, *Egyptian Ceramic Art,* 1898, p. 61, Fig. 133.
LENT BY: *Mr. Dikran G. Kelekian.*

119. WHITE GLASS LAMP for insertion in a polycandelon. Two groups of parallel lines incised on body. Glass now partly iridescent. Coptic. IVth-VIth Century. .253 m.

PROVENANCE: Unknown.

BIBLIOGRAPHY: Unpublished. For similar specimens see Emery, W. B., *The Royal Tombs of Ballana and Qustul*, Cairo, 1938, Vol. II, Pl. 106.

LENT BY: *The Brummer Gallery.*

*120. CYLINDRICAL BLOWN GLASS JUG. Amber glass with etched geometric decorations. Egyptian. IVth-Vth Century. .288 m.

PROVENANCE: Edfu.

BIBLIOGRAPHY: Harden, D. B., *Roman Glass from Karanis*, Ann Arbor, 1936, p. 255.

Wilbour Collection, Brooklyn Museum.

121. TERRA COTTA AMPULLA. Decorated in relief on both sides with St. Menas, frontal, orans, flanked by kneeling camels and crosses. Coptic. About Vth-VIIth Century. .11 x .075 m.

PROVENANCE: Unknown.

BIBLIOGRAPHY: Unpublished.

Wilbour Collection, Brooklyn Museum.

122. TERRA COTTA AMPULLA. Observe, St. Menas, frontal and nimbed, orans, flanked by camels. Reverse, Coptic inscription within wreath. Coptic. About Vth-VIIth Century. .08 m. (height).

PROVENANCE: Unknown.

BIBLIOGRAPHY: Unpublished.

Wilbour Collection, Brooklyn Museum.

123. POTTERY FRAGMENT. Red body with female head painted in black-brown. Coptic. VIth-VIIth Century. .085 x .245 m.

PROVENANCE: Unknown.

BIBLIOGRAPHY: Unpublished.

LENT BY: *The Brummer Gallery.*

*124. RED POTTERY DISH. White slip on rim and interior. Four fish painted on interior in black and red. Conventionalized grapevine below rim. Coptic. About VIth-VIIth Century. .124 x .475 m.

PROVENANCE: Unknown.

BIBLIOGRAPHY: Unpublished.

LENT BY: *The Brummer Gallery.*

*125. RED POTTERY VASE. On body, in black, animals and birds. Coptic.
VIth-VIIth Century.   .284 m.
PROVENANCE: Unknown.
BIBLIOGRAPHY: Unpublished.
LENT BY: *Mr. Dikran G. Kelekian.*

*126. PAINTED TERRA COTTA FEMALE FIGURINE. High triangular
headdress, pierced. Probably a funerary statuette. Hollow base. Coptic.
About VIth-VIIth Century.   .134 m.
PROVENANCE: Unknown. Purchased by Charles Edwin Wilbour in Egypt in
1883.
BIBLIOGRAPHY: Unpublished.
Wilbour Collection, Brooklyn Museum.

*127. PAINTED TERRA COTTA FEMALE FIGURINE. Possibly intended
to represent an orans.   Same type as preceding example. Coptic. VIth-
VIIth Century.   .145 m.
PROVENANCE: Unknown. Purchased by Charles Edwin Wilbour in Egypt in
1889.
BIBLIOGRAPHY: Unpublished.
Wilbour Collection, Brooklyn Museum.

128. **GOLD EARRINGS.** High, gold wire hook joining to hollow half globe. Disk with globules covers joining of hook to globe. Roman type. Ist-IInd Century. .028 m.

PROVENANCE: Unknown.

BIBLIOGRAPHY: Unpublished. The type is found frequently on Fayum portraits. *Brooklyn Museum Collection.*

129. **GOLD PENDANT.** In repoussé, a Serapis bust. Egypto-Roman. IInd-IIIrd (?) Century. .043 m.

PROVENANCE: Unknown.

BIBLIOGRAPHY: Unpublished. Cf. *Arch. Anz.*, 1909, p. 142, Fig. 1 (IInd Century A. D.?).

LENT BY: *Walters Art Gallery.*

*130. **GOLD CHAIN OF PLAITED WIRE.** At ends, hook and loop. Drop pendant in openwork. Roman type. IIIrd-Vth Century. .81 m.

PROVENANCE: Unknown. Purchased by Charles Edwin Wilbour at Bedresheyn, Egypt, in April, 1884.

BIBLIOGRAPHY: Unpublished.

Wilbour Collection, Brooklyn Museum.

Detail only illustrated.

*131. **GOLD WIRE CHAIN.** At ends, openwork disk and a hook. Central circular pendant with busts in repoussé of Isis and Horus. Egypto-Roman. Probably IIIrd Century. Length of chain, .375 m. Diameter of pendant, .056 m.

PROVENANCE: Unknown.

BIBLIOGRAPHY: Unpublished.

LENT BY: *Walters Art Gallery.*

*132. **GOLD AND PEARL NECKLACE.** Hollow gold doves separated by single pearls on gold wires. At ends, oval disk with incised concentric circles. Coptic. About IVth-Vth Century. .575 m.

PROVENANCE: Said to be from Nazareth.

BIBLIOGRAPHY: Unpublished.

LENT BY: *Mr. Robert Garrett.*

Detail only illustrated.

133.   CIRCULAR GLASS AMULET.   Light blue glass background.   Monogram of Christ inlaid in yellow glass within border of red and yellow circles. Suspension loop. Coptic. Probably IVth-Vth Century. .029 m.
PROVENANCE: Unknown.
BIBLIOGRAPHY: Unpublished.   For duplicate specimen see Petrie, W. M. F., *Amulets,* London, 1914, Pl. XLIV, No. 137aa.
Brooklyn Museum Collection.

134.   GOLD EARRINGS.   Intertwisted gold wire loop.   Soldered to loop, three rings of plain and beaded wire with pyramidal pellet decorations. Coptic (?).   About Vth-VIth Century.   .038 m. (diameter).
PROVENANCE: Unknown.
BIBLIOGRAPHY: Unpublished.
Brooklyn Museum Collection.

135.   GOLD EARRINGS.   Hollow gold loop.   Soldered to loop, two rings of plain and beaded wire with pyramidal pellet decorations.   In center, a hollow boss from which originally hung a gold wire with bead.   Coptic (?).   About Vth-VIth Century.   .036 m. (diameter).
PROVENANCE: Unknown.
BIBLIOGRAPHY: Unpublished.
Brooklyn Museum Collection.

*136.   GOLD EARRINGS.   Intertwisted gold wire loop.   Soldered to loop, three openwork discs with pyramidal pellet decorations on circumferences.   Coptic (?).   About Vth-VIth Century.   Greatest diameter, .04 m.
PROVENANCE: Unknown.
BIBLIOGRAPHY: Unpublished.
Brooklyn Museum Collection.

137.   GOLD EARRINGS.   Hollow gold loop.   Soldered to loop, two rings of tubular and beaded wire.   Coptic (?).   About Vth-VIth Century. .028 m. (diameter).
PROVENANCE: Unknown.
BIBLIOGRAPHY: Unpublished.
Brooklyn Museum Collection.

*138.   GOLD EARRING.   Circular hollow loop.   Pendant, a ring of tubular and twisted wire with pyramidal decorations of flattened pellets around rim. Below, a hollow boss and rod. Coptic. VIth Century. .046 m. (diameter).

PROVENANCE: Unknown.

BIBLIOGRAPHY: Unpublished.

Brooklyn Museum Collection.

*139. GOLD EARRINGS. Hollow gold loop. Soldered to loop, a hollow bi-conical pendant with beading at base. Below, green glass bead. Coptic. Probably VIth Century. .04 x .03 m. (diameter).

PROVENANCE: Unknown.

BIBLIOGRAPHY: Unpublished.

Brooklyn Museum Collection.

For a sculpture showing similar earrings, see Duthuit, *La Sculpture copte,* Pl. XXXII (a).

*140. GOLD EARRINGS. Duplicates of the preceding pair excepting shape of the pendant. Coptic. Probably VIth Century. .032 x .02 m. (diameter).

PROVENANCE: Unknown.

BIBLIOGRAPHY: Unpublished.

Brooklyn Museum Collection.

*141. STONE MOULD. Probably for making earrings. About Vth-VIIth (?) Century. Coptic. .038 x .082 m.

PROVENANCE: Unknown.

BIBLIOGRAPHY: Unpublished.

LENT BY: *Johns Hopkins University Archaeological Museum.*

*142. STEATITE MOULD. For small cross with suspension loop. About Vth-VIIth Century. Coptic. .044 x .022 m.

PROVENANCE: Unknown.

BIBLIOGRAPHY: Unpublished.

LENT BY: *Johns Hopkins University Archaeological Museum.*

143. STEATITE MOULD. For making metal amulets. Reverse, cross within a circle with suspension loop. Obverse, conventionalized crucifixion. Cross surmounted by bust of Christ and flanked by two saints (repro-duced on cover of catalogue). Coptic. After the Vth Century. .073 x .039 m.

PROVENANCE: Unknown. Acquired in Egypt by Charles Edwin Wilbour in 1886.

BIBLIOGRAPHY: Unpublished. Possibly a unique example.

Wilbour Collection, Brooklyn Museum.

44

Egyptian Textiles of the Graeco-Roman
and Early Christian Period

O<small>F ALL THE REMAINS</small> of the civilization of Egypt during the early centuries of our era, the textiles are the most abundant. Perhaps, also, they are in many ways the most revealing. They reflect the life of the period in an extraordinarily vivid manner, showing not only what people wore but also, to a limited extent, how they lived and what they thought about. The quality of the weaves is witness to a wide divergence of tastes and skills; their designs tell much of the religious and cultural background of the age and testify to the constant passing to and fro of people and ideas from one part to another of the great Roman Empire.

The cemeteries of Egypt have yielded the grave clothes of rich and poor, of pagan and Christian, of the city-bred aristocrat, of the vulgar bourgeois, of the uncultivated, often uncouth, populace. If we can judge from pictured representations from other parts of the Roman world, on mosaics, on ivories and in sculpture, the garments found in Egypt represent the contemporary fashions throughout the Roman Empire, a mingling of Mediterranean and Oriental dress, which was in vogue, with perhaps certain minor variations, wherever the legions held sway. There is little —almost nothing—that is native Egyptian either in style of dress or in its decoration.

Woven ornaments of the garments, coverlets and hangings (the two last probably used as shrouds or as covers thrown over coffins) often reflect two great arts of the period, mosaics and painting. Of mosaics, many examples have been preserved, but little has been done in the way of scientific comparison of textile designs with extant mosaics. The beautiful textile from the St. Louis City Art Museum, No. 182 of this catalogue (to name one example only among the textiles which suggest mosaic in color and pattern), may well have been inspired by a mosaic pavement, which itself may in turn have simulated a woven floor covering. Certain textiles suggest wall paintings: for instance, the fine head from the Detroit Museum (No. 231 of this catalogue); the head of St. Theodore, from the Fogg Museum (No. 243); the fragment of the Judgment of Paris belonging to Mr. Kevorkian (No. 235); and the boy with the duck belonging to Mr. Kelekian (No. 232). Others, such as the portrait head from the Cooper Union Museum (No. 206) and the portrait head from the Metropolitan Museum of Art (No. 184.), seem to be reflections of panel paintings. The purely ornamental designs, vine scrolls, repeat designs of floral and animal motifs, medallions containing busts, etc., were part of a universal grammar of ornament, used on carved stones (a number of reliefs in the exhibition show patterns used also on textiles), on frescoes, on mosaics, and in the so-called minor arts. Dr. Maurice Dimand, in his valuable book, *Die Ornamentik der ägyptischen Wollwerkereien*, has shown that some of these ornamental motifs were borrowed from a foreign, Near Eastern grammar of ornament. And a study of later Western art reveals how many of them journeyed down into the Early Christian and Medieval art of Europe.

While part of the ornament and a number of the pictorial representations on Egyptian textiles were inspired by Eastern originals, particularly by silk weaves from Sasanid Persia, perhaps more were derived from late Classical art. The textiles often echo very ancient motifs (cf. note to No. 193 of this catalogue, on the textile with the Centaur). Some of them illustrate tales of Classical mythology or portray, more or less clearly, pagan gods and goddesses; a few show scenes connected with the mystery cults that played so large a part in the religious life of the Graeco-Roman world.

The prevalence of pagan scenes well down into the sixth century may signify that paganism survived much longer, especially in the city-culture of Alexandria and in centers of Greek population elsewhere in Egypt, than is often conceded. It may also signify merely that many Christians wore garments with representations that had lost all save a purely literary significance. The old religion may have been outworn, but the old culture was for long the only culture available. With the exception of the Gospels, the literature of Early Christian Egypt was confined to sermons and hymns and naïve tales of martyrdom, generally undistinguished in style and content. "Higher" education rested on the foundation of the Classics; and a Classical repertoire of subjects in art can conceivably have been adopted, even by Christians, without any violence to their belief.

46

That it was so adopted is proved by the presence of pagan subjects in the architectural ornament of Christian edifices. To what extent these subjects had a symbolic Christian significance opens up a large field for speculation. That some of them acquired a symbolic meaning is beyond doubt, but at what stage they passed from their traditional place in the repertoire of ancient subjects into their new field of mystic meaning is not always clear. For example, the stags (Nos. 246 and 256), shown in the group of "Textiles with Christian Subjects," may in reality have been used merely as ornament without the slightest symbolic connotation. The stag fascinated by the serpent in No. 257, on the other hand, must have been used symbolically.

Certain it is that the early Christians of Egypt, like their descendants of today, were not of an austere and simple faith. Literary remains reveal a long struggle to reconcile the teachings of Jesus with old beliefs and superstitions dear to the hearts of the Egyptians. The tunic panel in the Brooklyn Museum Collection (No. 255 of this exhibition), with the woven representation of a cross on a jeweled chain and, in the V formed by the chain, a nude female dancing figure, may be a witness of this struggle. At least, Strzygowski speculates as to whether this combination of the nude figure with the cross, which appears fairly frequently, may not be one of the symbols of the Gnostic heresy (*Koptische Kunst*, p. 278, No. 9101).

Of textiles with unmistakably Christian ornament, relatively few, in comparison with the vast quantity preserved, are known. A number are represented in the exhibition. The head of St. Theodore (No. 243) shows that fine weaves with Christian subjects must have existed, though the majority of those that have come down to us (with the exception of a few silk weaves of uncertain provenance) are crude examples of the weaver's art. Most of the Christian textiles are monotonous repetitions of saints, undistinguishable one from the other and crudely woven in savage colors. The looped figure of a saint from the Textile Museum of the District of Columbia (No. 249) is a notable exception. Occasionally, a clear example of a Biblical scene presents itself. Such is the woven picture of the Sacrifice of Isaac from the Cooper Union Museum (No. 253). The same museum also possesses a very coarse tapestry weave that represents the visit of the Magi, and a textile from the collection of Mr. Walter Hauser on exhibition in the Metropolitan Museum of Art shows incidents from the story of Joseph. The large ornamental hangings of the Kevorkian Collection (No. 262 and No. 263) may have been altar hangings from early churches. No. 263 is particularly interesting as a rare example of an early resist-dyed fabric.

The textiles in this collection are for the most part tapestry-woven woolen ornaments cut from linen or woolen garments. Included also are a few loom-woven patterned woolen fabrics, some pieces with so-called "inlaid" designs, their patterns brocaded into the warps, several looped fabrics made, roughly, in somewhat the same manner as modern velvets, and a small number of silk weaves, very rare in Egypt, especially during the earlier periods. An ideal catalogue would discuss materials, weaves and dyes in detail. But such a task is a matter of months, if not years, of special research. Some work has recently been done toward studying technique as a guide to provenance and date. M. Pfister, for example, has done valuable research in the weaves and dyes of Coptic textiles. While some of his conclusions on provenance seem perhaps a bit premature, he has certainly pointed the way to a more scientific examination of textiles, which may be of great assistance, as more material is made available, in determining their period and origin.

All of which brings us to two great problems of the so-called "Coptic" textiles and to the inevitable apology which must accompany every catalogue.

First comes the question of provenance. It seems clear that some of the textiles found in Egyptian cemeteries must have been imports from Syria or Persia. It is beyond doubt that many of them, even if woven in Egypt, were inspired by models from farther East. I have not attempted any speculation as to ultimate provenance—not even the usual "Egypt or Syria?". It seems reasonable to assume some imports, and equally reasonable to assume that very fine textiles were produced in Egypt, down to the latest years before the Mohammadan conquest, as they were in the early years of the Islamic period. Egypt had a long tradition of fine weaving, and even in the centuries of unrest that preceded the Arab invasions there must have been always a certain number, varying with economic conditions, of persons willing and able to pay for textiles of good quality. The tendency to believe that all finer weaves originated outside of Egypt and that, especially in the latter part of the pre-Islamic period, only the coarser in texture and cruder in pattern could have been of local manufacture, seems to me without sure foundation.

Likewise unwarranted seems the dating of the textiles from Egypt on the basis of design or weave or subject matter alone. Which brings us to the second problem—that of dating. It is generally agreed that few textiles can be earlier than the middle of the third century. From that early date, crude textiles can have been and undoubtedly were produced by unskilled or provincial weavers simultaneously with fine textiles produced for discriminating customers in the urban centers. Skill of weave or design is therefore no absolute criterion. Nor, within certain limits, is subject matter. As I have suggested, Classical subjects seem to have persisted much later than was once believed possible, though I think it is safe to admit that they vanished from Egypt, along with the civilization that produced them, after the Arab conquest. In the early years of Islam, the whole aspect of Egyptian textiles changes. Even those that carry on old motifs have a new and unmistakable character.

Of course the whole question of dating has still to be answered, and I do not pretend to have answered it adequately. Our positive information from excavation is very scant; there has been little really scientific excavation of the cemeteries and rubbish heaps from which the textiles come. The Brooklyn Museum possesses a group of a hundred-odd excavated fragments from Antinoë. According to the excavation records of the Egypt Exploration Society, they are of the sixth century, a few perhaps of the late fifth. On the basis of style, they run almost the whole gamut of design, from the skilfully woven classic, to the disarticulated, crude, mistaken designs generally regarded as an earmark of the late period. A few of them show Christian subjects—the cross (No. 244) and the acrostic and the stag (Nos. 245 and 246), both of which may or may not be Christian—and a few show Persian patterns coarsely interpreted.

To summarize, the whole field of Egyptian textiles demands a more thorough study of techniques and dyes and iconographic and ornamental types. There must be comparison of textile remains with other monuments of the period, and with pieces from reliable excavations before the final word on the origin and dating can be said. In the meantime this catalogue suggests dates which may or may not stand the test of future research. Where the dating differs from that of the lenders of the pieces, the substitution has been made merely in the interest of consistency.

I wish to acknowledge my indebtedness to Professor Lehmann-Hartleben of New York University for his help in identifying certain of the classical representations. I am most grateful also to Dr. Walter Federn for suggested readings of the Coptic inscriptions. And, finally, I am most of all indebted to the many lenders, who have been so generous in giving, not only the textiles themselves but also the notes and measurements and photographs on which, in large part, this catalogue is based.

Elizabeth Riefstahl
Charles Edwin Wilbour
Memorial Library

SHORT BIBLIOGRAPHY

Apostolaki, Annes: *The Coptic Weaves in the Athens Museum of Decorative Arts.* Athens, Typographer "Estia", 1932. (In Greek).

British Museum: *A Guide to the Early Christian and Byzantine Antiquities,* by G. M. Dalton. 2nd ed. London, 1921.

Butler, Alfred J.: *The Ancient Coptic Churches of Egypt.* Oxford, Clarendon pr., 1884. 2 v.

Dalton, Ormand M.: *Byzantine Art and Archaeology.* Oxford, Clarendon pr., 1911.

Dimand, Maurice S.: *Coptic Tunics in the Metropolitan Museum of Art.* New York, Metropolitan Museum of Art, 1930. (In *Metropolitan Museum Studies,* v. 2, pt. 2, p. 239-252)

Die Ornamentik der ägyptischen Wollwirkereien. Leipzig, J. C. Hinrichs, 1924.

See also articles by Dimand in the *Bulletin of the Metropolitan Museum of Art,* especially v. 21, 25, 26; 1926, 1930, 1931.

Errera, Mme Isabella: *Collection d' anciennes étoffes égyptiennes.* Bruxelles, Imprimerie J. E. Goossens, 1916.

Falke, Otto v.: *Kunstgeschichte der Seidenweberei.* Berlin, E. Wasmuth, 1913. 2 v.

Forrer, Robert: *Die frühchristlichen Alterthümer aus dem Gräberfelde von Achmim-Panopolis.* Strassburg, 1893.

Gayet, Albert Jean: *Le Costume en Égypte du IIIe au XIIIe siècle.* Paris, Leroux, 1900. (Paris. Exposition Universelle. Palais du Costume).

Gerspach, Edouard: *Les Tapisseries coptes.* Paris, Quantin, 1890.

Grüneisen, Vladimir de: *Les Caractéristiques de l'art copte.* Florence, Fratelli Alénari, 1922.

Kelekian, Dikran G.: *Important Documents of Coptic Art in the Collection of Dikran G. Kelekian.* New York [1929].

Kendrick, Albert F.: *Catalogue of Textiles from Burying Grounds in Egypt.* London, H. M. Stationery off., 1920-22. 3 v.

See also articles by Kendrick in the *Burlington Magazine,* especially v. 31-32, 48; 1916-17, 1926.

Lessing, Julius: *Die Gewebe-Sammlung des K. Kunstgewerbe-Museum.* Berlin, E. Wasmuth, 1900. v. 1.

Morey, Charles R.: *The Mosaics of Antioch.* London, Longmans, Green and co., 1938.

Peirce, Hayford and Tyler, Royall: *L'Art byzantin.* Paris, Librairie de France, 1932-34. 2 v.

Pfister, R.: *Textiles de Palmyre.* Paris, Les Editions d'art et d'histoire, 1934-40. 3 v.

Tissus coptes du Musée du Louvre. Paris, H. Ernst [1932].

See also articles by Pfister in *Revue des arts asiatiques,* v. 5-8, 1930-33.

Riegl, Alois: *Die ägyptischen Textilfunde im K. K. Osterreich. Museum.* Vienna, Waldheim, 1889.

Tapisseries et étoffes coptes. Paris, H. Ernst [n.d.].

Wulff, Oskar K. and Volbach, Wolfgang F.: *Spätantike und koptische Stoffe aus ägyptischen Grabfunden in den Staatlichen Museen.* Berlin, E. Wasmuth, [1926]. (Veröffentlichung der Staatlichen Museen.)

TEXTILES WITH GEOMETRICAL MOTIFS

144. **CIRCLE WITH INTERLACINGS.** Purple wool tapestry weave with interlacing forming lozenges in undyed linen thread. Border of fruits and leaves. IIIrd-IVth Century. Diameter, 28.5 cm.
PROVENANCE: Unknown.
BIBLIOGRAPHY: Unpublished.
Brooklyn Museum Collection.

*145. **SQUARE WITH INTERLACING.** Tapestry-woven in purple wool with intricate interlacing forming fine design of star and octagonal rosette in undyed linen thread. Border with undulated vine. IIIrd-IVth Century. 39.7 x 33 cm.
PROVENANCE: Unknown.
BIBLIOGRAPHY: Unpublished.
Brooklyn Museum Collection.
     This design later becomes a favorite motif of Islamic interlaced ornament.

*146. **SQUARE WITH GEOMETRICAL DESIGN.** Tapestry-woven in purple wool with fine design in undyed linen thread. Border of conventionalized plant design. IIIrd-IVth Century. 37.5 x 37 cm.
PROVENANCE: Unknown.
BIBLIOGRAPHY: Unpublished.
Collection of the New York Historical Society in the Brooklyn Museum.
     Such large geometrical ornaments may have been used on hangings or on the cloak, or pallium, which was part of the costume of the period.

147. **STAR-SHAPED ORNAMENT.** Tapestry-woven in purple and orange-yellow wool and undyed linen thread into a plain linen cloth. In the center, a gazelle and, in the angles formed by the star, conventionalized grape leaves. IVth-Vth Century. 38 x 30 cm.
PROVENANCE: Unknown.
BIBLIOGRAPHY: Unpublished.
LENT BY: *Pratt Institute.*

*148. **GEOMETRICAL STAR.** Tapestry-woven in purple wool and undyed linen into undyed woolen cloth. Ornamented with central roundel containing guilloche and, in the angles formed by the points of the star, ivy leaves. Ivy leaves issue from between the points into the field of the textile. IVth-Vth Century. Diameter, 21 cm.
PROVENANCE: Unknown.
BIBLIOGRAPHY: Unpublished.
LENT BY: *Textile Museum of the District of Columbia.*

149. **STRIP WITH "INLAID" DESIGN.** Lozenge pattern in colored wool, not embroidered, but laid in (by a method similar to brocading) while the cloth is on the loom. Vth-VIth Century. 78 x 16 cm.
PROVENANCE: Unknown.
BIBLIOGRAPHY: Unpublished.
LENT BY: *Pratt Institute.*

150. **SQUARE WITH GEOMETRIC DESIGN.** Interlacing and lozenge patterns in five compartments. Border of "Greek wave". VIth-VIIth Century. 14 cm. square.
PROVENANCE: Unknown. (Baron Collection)
BIBLIOGRAPHY: Unpublished.
LENT BY: *Cooper Union Museum.*

151. **PART OF TUNIC.** Clavus and square ornament in purple wool and undyed linen tapestry-woven into yellow wool cloth on wool warps. VIth-VIIth Century. 38.5 x 68 cm.
PROVENANCE: Unknown.
BIBLIOGRAPHY: Unpublished.
LENT BY: *Textile Museum of the District of Columbia.*

54

*152. TAPESTRY WITH POMEGRANATE TREE. Fragment of a large hanging showing part of pomegranate tree with fruit. The stems are in pale purple, the leaves in two shades of green with yellowish veins, the fruits salmon-red with yellowish high lights, the background deep blue. Wool tapestry, woven into a plain, not very fine linen cloth. IIIrd-IVth Century. 39 x 50.5 cm.

PROVENANCE: Unknown.

BIBLIOGRAPHY: Unpublished.

LENT BY: *Cooper Union Museum.*

One of the most striking specimens of late Classic weaving, almost comparable in color and skill to certain medieval tapestries. Particularly interesting is the twisting of the warps to conform with the design.

*153. TAPESTRY WITH FLOWERING SHRUB. Ornamental motif, probably from a large hanging, showing tree with flame-colored blossoms. The leaves are in two shades of green and the branches pale red. IIIrd-IVth Century. 56 x 26.2 cm.

PROVENANCE: Unknown.

BIBLIOGRAPHY: Unpublished.

LENT BY: *Mr. and Mrs. William R. Tyler.*

This rare Egyptian tapestry weave is comparable to the preceding number from Cooper Union in both style and technique. It may represent the pomegranate tree in blossom, as the Cooper Union piece represents it in fruit. See Dimand, *Ornamentik,* p. 64, for discussion of the pomegranate motif.

*154. LARGE VINE MOTIF. Tapestry-woven in deep blue wool and undyed linen into plain linen cloth. Bold pattern of stems and attached leaves and grapes. IVth Century. 57.1 x 53.4 cm.

PROVENANCE: Unknown.

BIBLIOGRAPHY: Unpublished.

LENT BY: *Boston Museum of Fine Arts.*

Probably from a hanging. An identical piece in Berlin Museum (Wulff-Volbach, pl. 64).

155. BAND WITH UNDULATED VINE. Graceful design of conventionalized ivy in wool and undyed linen. IVth-Vth Century. 16.5 x 3 cm.

PROVENANCE: Unknown.

BIBLIOGRAPHY: Unpublished.

LENT BY: *Pratt Institute.*

156. **BAND WITH HEART-SHAPED LEAVES.** Center ornamented in bold pattern, purple on white ground, flanked by slightly narrower borders of undulated bands, orange on purple ground, which form diamond-shaped compartments containing four-lobed rosettes outlined in undyed linen thread. Tapestry-woven in linen cloth of good quality. IVth-Vth Century. 49.5 x 24 cm.

PROVENANCE: Unknown.

BIBLIOGRAPHY: Unpublished.

LENT BY: *Pratt Institute.*

*157. **VINE GROWING FROM URN.** Design in wool and undyed linen tapestry weave shows deep blue vine with hare and bird in the branches. Gadrooned urn and clusters of fruit are red; pale greenish blue high light on urn. IVth-Vth Century. 21.5 x 16.5 cm.

PROVENANCE: Unknown.

BIBLIOGRAPHY: Unpublished.

LENT BY: *Pratt Institute.*

One of the most graceful motifs of Coptic textile art. Cf. examples in the Victoria and Albert Museum (Kendrick, *Catalogue*, v. I., p. 88, pl. XXIII).

Cooper Union Museum possesses a particularly fine example.

*158. **BORDER WITH GRAPEVINE MOTIF.** Vine forms oval cartouches with semi-naturalistic vine leaves and tendrils attached. Tapestry-woven in purple wool and undyed linen. IVth-Vth Century. 48 x 8.5 cm.

PROVENANCE: Unknown.

BIBLIOGRAPHY: *Brooklyn museum quarterly,* v. XVI, 1929, p. 52.

LENT BY: *Pratt Institute.*

*159. **SQUARE WITH HARE IN FOLIAGE.** Tapestry-woven. The hare is realistically rendered in purple wool with orange-yellow eye. The foliage green with red fruit. Handsome acanthus border. IVth-Vth Century. 21 cm. square.

PROVENANCE: Unknown.

BIBLIOGRAPHY: Unpublished.

LENT BY: *Pratt Institute.*

A similar square is in the Boston Museum of Fine Arts (acc. no. 96.343 b). Another is in the Victoria and Albert Museum (Kendrick, *Catalogue*, v. I. p. 138, pl. XXIV).

160. **BAND WITH ANIMALS IN ACANTHUS SCROLLS.** Lively design tapestry-woven in purple-red wool and undyed linen. IVth-Vth Century. 43 x 7.5 cm.

PROVENANCE: Unknown.
BIBLIOGRAPHY: Unpublished.
LENT BY: *Pratt Institute.*

*161. **RABBIT EATING GRAPES.** The animal, in purple-brown wool with details in undyed linen, nibbling orange grapes on a green stem. Tapestry-woven into plain linen cloth. IVth-Vth Century. 24 x 29 cm.
PROVENANCE: Unknown.
BIBLIOGRAPHY: Unpublished.
LENT BY: *Philadelphia Museum of Art.*

162. **BAND WITH RUNNING ANIMALS.** Lion and bull set in linked medallions. Tapestry-woven in purple wool on undyed linen ground, with border showing lanceolate leaves in red and green on undulated vine. Vth Century. 45 x 23.5 cm.
PROVENANCE: Unknown.
BIBLIOGRAPHY: Unpublished.
LENT BY: *Pratt Institute.*

*163. **SQUARE WITH FRUIT BASKET.** Conventionalized basket set in center of an octagonal cartouche ornamented with floral motifs. Coarsely tapestry-woven in colored wools and undyed linen thread into coarse plain linen cloth. Vth Century. 29 x 30 cm.
PROVENANCE: Unknown.
BIBLIOGRAPHY: Unpublished.
Brooklyn Museum Collection.

164. **BASKET WITH FRUIT AND LEAVES.** A semi-naturalistic rendering, forming the central motif of a square bordered with a guilloche. Tapestry-woven in brilliantly polychromed wool and undyed linen, into a coarse plain linen cloth. Vth Century. 20 x 27 cm.
PROVENANCE: Unknown.
BIBLIOGRAPHY: Unpublished.
LENT BY: *Professor Vladimir G. Simkhovitch.*

165. **POLYCHROMED BAND.** Design of fruit baskets and leaves set alternately in oval compartments formed by conventionalized leaf motifs

tapestry-woven in plain linen cloth.   Vivid coloring with red and green predominating.   Vth Century.   113 x 21 cm. (band).

PROVENANCE: Unknown.

BIBLIOGRAPHY: Unpublished.

LENT BY: *Pratt Institute.*

  Probably part of a hanging.

166.   FLORAL BAND.   Boldly polychromed band tapestry-woven in colored wools and undyed linen.   Undulated yellow border.   Vth Century.   21 x 96 cm.

PROVENANCE: Unknown.

BIBLIOGRAPHY: Unpublished.

LENT BY: *Textile Museum of the District of Columbia.*

167.   PARROT IN NATURALISTIC COLORS.   Probably a portion of a hanging.   Tapestry-woven in colored wools into very coarse linen cloth. Vth-VIth Century.   20 x 11.5 cm.

PROVENANCE: Unknown.

BIBLIOGRAPHY: Unpublished.

LENT BY: *Pratt Institute.*

168.   SQUARE WITH HARE.   Hare in central roundel.   Purple-black wool and undyed linen.   Vth-VIth Century.   11.5 cm. square.

PROVENANCE: Unknown. (Baron Collection)

BIBLIOGRAPHY: Unpublished.

LENT BY: *Cooper Union Museum.*

169.   ANIMALS IN LANDSCAPE.   Looped technique in colored wools on plain linen.   Rather free composition of animals among trees.   Vth-VIth Century.   100 x 53 cm.

PROVENANCE: Unknown.

BIBLIOGRAPHY: Unpublished.

LENT BY: *Textile Museum of the District of Columbia.*

*170.   "BROCADED" CLOTH.   Repeat design of wreaths and lobed rosettes in white linen "brocading" on red ground.   VIth Century.   24 x 40 cm.

PROVENANCE: Unknown.

BIBLIOGRAPHY: Unpublished.

Brooklyn Museum Collection.

171. WOOLEN WEAVE IMITATING SILK FABRIC. Fine tapestry weave in rich polychromy. Stripes of varying widths ornamented with conventionalized palmettes, scrolled cartouches, etc. VIth Century. 34 x 27 cm.
PROVENANCE: Unknown.
BIBLIOGRAPHY: Unpublished.
LENT BY: *Professor Vladimir G. Simkhovitch.*

*172. TAPESTRY-WOVEN BAND. From a woolen tunic. Design of roundels with attached spirals forming smaller roundels. The small roundels contain birds and the large, birds, animals, portrait heads and human figures. VIth Century. 23 x 84 cm.
PROVENANCE: Unknown.
BIBLIOGRAPHY: Unpublished.
Brooklyn Museum Collection.

*173. SQUARE WITH LIONS AND EAGLE. The square, tapestry-woven in black wool and undyed linen thread, is divided into four compartments; two contain seated lions with heads turned back toward center and an eagle poised above them, and two contain octagonal stars formed of interlaced bands. VIth-VIIth Century. 14.5 cm. square.
PROVENANCE: Unknown.
BIBLIOGRAPHY: Unpublished.
LENT BY: *Pratt Institute.*

*174. LIONS COPIED FROM SILK WEAVE. Roundel with confronted lions of heraldic style. Tapestry weave of colored wools and undyed linen on red ground with border on blue, set into woolen cloth. VIth-VIIth Century. 41 x 35 cm.
PROVENANCE: Unknown.
BIBLIOGRAPHY: Unpublished.
LENT BY: *Textile Museum of the District of Columbia.*

Compare silk weave (probably Byzantine of Sasanid inspiration) from Sancta Sanctorum, now in Vatican library (Dalton, *Byzantine Art*, p. 593, fig. 373); also, similar wool tapestry in Athens (Apostolaki, p. 171, fig. 738).

*175. LION COPIED FROM SILK WEAVE. Similar to the preceding. VIth-VIIth Century. 20 x 135 cm.
PROVENANCE: Unknown.
BIBLIOGRAPHY: Unpublished.
LENT BY: *Textile Museum of the District of Columbia.*

*176. LIONS CONFRONTING A DATE-PALM. Long border, the lion motif alternating with giraffes in roundels. Tapestry-woven in colored wools on yellow ground; woolen warps. VIIth Century. 20 x 135 cm.

PROVENANCE: Unknown.

BIBLIOGRAPHY: Unpublished.

LENT BY: *Textile Museum of the District of Columbia.*

Detail only illustrated.

*177. TREE FLANKED BY LIONS. The tree springs from an urn; the lions in heraldic soberness on either side. Tapestry-woven in richly colored wools and undyed linen on deep blue ground. VIth Century. 22 x 26 cm.

PROVENANCE: Unknown.

BIBLIOGRAPHY: Unpublished.

LENT BY: *Textile Museum of the District of Columbia.*

An unusually spirited copy of a motif from a Sasanid silk fabric. A similar piece, though not so fine, is in the Athens Museum (cf. Apostolaki, p. 169, fig. 139); another, on red ground, in the Berlin Museum (Wulff-Volbach, pl. 26).

*178. "TREE OF LIFE" WITH BIRDS. Brilliantly polychromed version of Sasanid motif of palmette with heraldic birds beneath it and in its leaves. Wool tapestry weave. VIth Century. 10.7 x 12 cm.

PROVENANCE: Unknown.

BIBLIOGRAPHY: Unpublished.

LENT BY: *Walters Art Gallery.*

179. DATE-PALM WITH DATES. Tapestry-woven in wool of richly somber tones and undyed linen. VIth-VIIth Century. 12 x 13 cm.

PROVENANCE: Unknown.

BIBLIOGRAPHY: Unpublished.

LENT BY: *Textile Museum of the District of Columbia.*

180. TAPESTRY-WOVEN BAND. Medallions with animals and plant motifs, in brilliant colors and undyed linen thread on red wool background. VIIth Century. 42 x 8.5 cm.

PROVENANCE: Unknown.

BIBLIOGRAPHY: Unpublished.

LENT BY: *Pratt Institute.*

*181. HUNTING SCENE. Plain compound woolen cloth on linen warps with lively, all-over design, green on red ground. Men on foot and horseback hunt lions, stags and leopards with spear, bow and arrow; the horsemen are attended by dogs. A tree suggests landscape. Edged with bands of green and purple. IIIrd-IVth Century. 36 x 20 cm.
PROVENANCE: Unknown.
BIBLIOGRAPHY: Unpublished.
LENT BY: *Philadelphia Museum of Art.*

An identical piece in the Berlin Museum (cf. Falke, v. I, p. 23-24, fig. 31, and, in color, Wulff-Volbach, pl. 36). This is a hunting scene in the late antique tradition, without Sasanid influence.

*182. PASTORAL SCENE. Shepherd milking a goat. Tapestry in deep blue and red wool and undyed linen. Border of birds in vines. Spirited and humorous rendering. IIIrd-IVth Century. 35 cm. square.
PROVENANCE: Said to be Akhmim.
BIBLIOGRAPHY: Whittemore, Thomas, Two Coptic cloths, in *Studies presented to F. LL. Griffith*, London, 1932, p. [384]-387, pl. 60.
LENT BY: *St. Louis City Art Museum.*

Such pastoral scenes were a favorite theme of late Classic art. Similar in subject are the silk roundels of the Hirsch collection (Worcester Museum catalogue *The Dark Ages*, no. 134-137), which have been aptly compared with the miniatures in the Vatican manuscript of the *Eclogues* of Virgil (Goldschmidt, Adolf, Exhibition of the art of the Dark Ages at the Worcester Art Museum, in *Parnassus*, v. 9, 1937, p. 29-30).

*183. HEAD OF A GODDESS. Medallion, with looping in colored wool, representing a divinity with a crescent-shaped ornament in her hair (Luna?). IIIrd-IVth Century. 56.5 x 45 cm.
PROVENANCE: Unknown.
BIBLIOGRAPHY: Unpublished.
LENT BY: *Metropolitan Museum of Art.*

This head represents the most skilful weaving in the looped technique. It has all the quality of a fine mosaic.

*184. HEAD OF CERES (?). Portrait head in fine tapestry weave of brilliantly colored wools. IVth Century. 24.5 x 22 cm.
PROVENANCE: Unknown.

BIBLIOGRAPHY: Unpublished.
LENT BY: *Metropolitan Museum of Art.*

This very fine example with flowers held in a drapery may represent the goddess Ceres or a season. Cf. the figures of the seasons in the Antioch mosaics with fruits held in a napkin (Morey, C. R. *The Mosaics of Antioch*, New York, 1938, pls. XVI and XVII).

*185. **BORDER WITH PORTRAIT HEADS.** Haloed heads separated by serrated leaves with palmette flowers tapestry-woven in brilliant polychromy on dark blue ground. IVth Century. 18 x 57 cm.

PROVENANCE: Unknown.

BIBLIOGRAPHY: Unpublished.

Brooklyn Museum Collection.

Such heads may represent deities, saints or personages. This example is probably of pagan origin; the halo has not necessarily any Christian significance. The piece is typical of much of the art of the period in its combination of Greek and Oriental characteristics. A fragment of an almost identical if not the same border is in the Boston Museum of Fine Arts (acc. no. 30.685).

186. **SQUARE WITH PORTRAIT HEADS.** Large tapestry-woven square in colored wool and white linen on deep blue ground. In the center and at the four corners, portrait heads, the latter separated by floral motifs. IVth Century. 30 x 33.5 cm.

PROVENANCE: Unknown.

BIBLIOGRAPHY: Unpublished.

LENT BY: *Mr. H. Kevorkian.*

A piece very similar in style to the preceding border.

*187. **BORDER WITH CLASSICAL FIGURES.** Tapestry-woven in purple wool and undyed linen. At top, haloed god, nude save for buskins and floating scarf, leans on a lance; a dog is at his feet. Below, separated by a roundel containing an amorino, a female figure in flowing garments dances to a lyre she holds in her hands. Border of lanceolate leaves. IVth Century. 6 x 105 cm.

PROVENANCE: Unknown.

BIBLIOGRAPHY: Unpublished.

LENT BY: *Textile Museum of the District of Columbia.*

Detail only illustrated.

188. **FIGURE OF A VICTOR** (?). Boldly rendered design of nude figure with cloak carrying palm branch (Victor ?). Tapestry-woven in black, brown and green wool and undyed linen. Figure apparently cut from hanging and mounted in modern times in roundel of looped cloth with vine border (cf. roundel with mask in Brooklyn Museum collection illustrated in this catalogue). IVth Century. Diameter, 50 cm.

PROVENANCE: Unknown.

BIBLIOGRAPHY: Kelekian, *Important documents of Coptic art*, New York, [1929].

LENT BY: *Mr. Dikran G. Kelekian.*

*189. **DEITY IN CHARIOT.** Known as the "Triumph of Bacchus". Panel, tapestry-woven in black wool and undyed linen, shows deity with crenellated crown standing in chariot drawn by lions or leopards. To right and left, female figures in flowing Greek costume, seemingly in divine frenzy. On the extreme left, Pan, and on the extreme right another male figure. The whole against a background ornamented with vine leaves. Composition skilfully fitted into a semi-circle with dolphins in the corners. IVth Century. 34 x 22 cm.

PROVENANCE: Unknown.

BIBLIOGRAPHY: Unpublished.

LENT BY: *Metropolitan Museum of Art.*

A piece remarkable for its fine rhythmic design and of great interest on account of its apparent connection with one of the mystery cults of the Eastern Roman Empire.

*190. **SWIMMING AMORINO WITH DOLPHIN.** Square in tapestry weave of deep purple wool and undyed linen. IVth-Vth Century. 12 cm. square.

PROVENANCE: Unknown.

BIBLIOGRAPHY: Unpublished.

LENT BY: *Pratt Institute.*

*191. **BAND WITH DANCING FIGURES.** Pairs of dancing figures with shields (Corybantes?) flank a central nude dancing figure (Maenad?). Tapestry-woven in purple wool (browned) and undyed linen thread. IVth-Vth Century. 18.5 x 34 cm.

PROVENANCE: Unknown.

BIBLIOGRAPHY: Unpublished.

LENT BY: *Pratt Institute.*

*192. WIDE BORDER FROM COVERLET OR GARMENT. Fine design of roundels formed by undulated vines. Each roundel contains slightly varying motifs, shrubs with birds or hares alternating with fighting animals and warriors, tapestry-woven in black wool and undyed linen thread. At one end, a boldly designed head in polychromy. IVth-Vth Century. 29 x 111 cm.

PROVENANCE: Unknown.
BIBLIOGRAPHY: Unpublished.
LENT BY: *Mme. Marguerite Mallon.*

*193. SQUARE WITH CENTAUR. Tapestry-woven in purple and colored wools on undyed linen ground. Vine-scrolls with attached leaves and fruit in green and red forming medallions. In the center medallion is the centaur, holding a laurel branch, a shield at his feet. The corner medallions show warriors with shield and wreath and winged horses. Between the medallions are baskets with fruits. IVth-Vth Century. 28.5 cm. square.

PROVENANCE: Unknown.
BIBLIOGRAPHY: *Brooklyn museum quarterly*, v. XVI, 1929, p. 53.
LENT BY: *Pratt Institute.*

The motifs of this textile—centaur, warrior, winged horse—are familiar subjects of Classic art. They can all be seen on a bronze plaque from Olympia (perhaps itself a copy of a textile design) dated in the VIIth Century, B. C. (cf. Gardiner, Norman, *Olympia*, Oxford, 1925, fig. 19). A similar square from Akhmim is in the Victoria and Albert Museum (Kendrick, *Catalogue*, v. I. p. 67, pl. XVII).

194. SQUARE WITH RUNNING FIGURES. Interlocked circles containing running figures against background with floral sprays. In the center, a bird. Tapestry-woven in black and undyed linen. IVth-Vth Century. 19 cm. square.

PROVENANCE: Unknown.
BIBLIOGRAPHY: Unpublished.
LENT BY: *Pratt Institute.*

*195. ROUNDEL WITH ORPHEUS AND EURYDICE(?). Tapestry-woven in black wool with touches of red and green and undyed linen thread. Nude male figure to the left leaning on a lyre; to the right, draped female figure. IVth-Vth Century. 48 x 51 cm.

PROVENANCE: Unknown.

BIBLIOGRAPHY: Unpublished.
LENT BY: *Walters Art Gallery.*

Could also be interpreted as Apollo and Daphnae, a subject familiar to Coptic art (cf. more realistic tapestry from Antinoë in the Musée Guimet, in *Tapisseries et étoffes coptes,* published by H. Ernst, Paris, n.d., pl. 42, and in Grüneisen, *Caracteristiques,* pl. XXIII).

196. **PERSONAGE MOUNTED ON PANTHER.** Tapestry-woven square, black wool and undyed linen. Central medallion with personage on panther (Dionysos?) surrounded by vine scrolls containing winged genii carrying baskets and ducks and, alternately, lions and hares. IVth-Vth Century. 17 cm. square.
PROVENANCE: Unknown. (Baron Collection)
BIBLIOGRAPHY: Unpublished.
LENT BY: *Cooper Union Museum.*

197. **PERSONAGE AND HARE.** Tapestry-woven square in black wool and undyed linen. IVth-Vth Century. 6 x 6.3 cm.
PROVENANCE: Unknown. (Baron Collection)
BIBLIOGRAPHY: Unpublished.
LENT BY: *Cooper Union Museum.*

A very similar piece, from Akhmim, in Errara, I., *Collection d'anciennes étoffes égyptiennes...* Brussels, 1916, p. 54, no. 123.

198. **ROUNDEL WITH WARRIOR.** Tapestry-woven in black wool and undyed linen. IVth-Vth Century. Diameter, 7.6 cm.
PROVENANCE: Unknown. (Miquel y Badia Collection)
BIBLIOGRAPHY: Unpublished.
LENT BY: *Cooper Union Museum.*

199. **FRAGMENT OF BORDER.** Nude female figure with bowl and ewer of sacrifice. Purple wool and undyed linen, tapestry-woven into looped linen cloth. IVth-Vth Century. 9 x 16.5 cm.
PROVENANCE: Unknown. (Baron Collection)
BIBLIOGRAPHY: Unpublished.
LENT BY: *Cooper Union Museum.*

200. **BORDER WITH CLASSICAL FIGURE.** Tapestry-woven in blue-black wool and undyed linen. IVth-Vth Century. 5.7 x 16.5 cm.
PROVENANCE: Unknown. (Baron Collection)

BIBLIOGRAPHY: Unpublished.
LENT BY: *Cooper Union Museum.*

*201.   SILK SQUARE WITH HORSEMAN.   Horseman in central circle;
border with water-birds, fish, ducks and plant motifs.   Tapestry-woven
in colored silk on green ground.   Linen warp.   IVth-Vth Century.   9.8
cm. square.
PROVENANCE: Unknown.
BIBLIOGRAPHY: Unpublished.
LENT BY: *Boston Museum of Fine Arts.*

      An identical specimen in the Victoria and Albert Museum (Kendrick,
Catalogue, v. I, p. 66, pl. XIV, and Dalton, *Byzantine art,* p. 81, fig. 46, who
dates it VIth Century).   A very similar square, in wool, in the Musée des Arts
Decoratifs, Paris (Carnot, Tapis et tapisseries de l'Orient, in *l'Illustration,* Dec.
1, 1934).   A Roman mosaic found at Sheikh Zuede, in the Arabian desert, on
the ancient caravan route between Egypt and Syria, in a fortress said to date
from 168 to 361 A.D., has a strikingly similar border (Clédat, in *Annales du
service des antiquités,* v. 15, 1915, pl. V).

202.   BORDER WITH NUDE FIGURE.   Highly conventionalized figure
and remains of roundel with lion.   Purple-black wool and undyed linen.
IVth-Vth Century.   4.75 x 16 cm.
PROVENANCE: Unknown. (Baron Collection)
BIBLIOGRAPHY: Unpublished.
LENT BY: *Cooper Union Museum.*

203.   AMORINI IN ROUNDELS.   Fragment of square, showing two border
motifs of amorini in vine scrolls, with fruit basket in between.   Tapestry-
woven in black wool and undyed linen thread, with touches of red and
green.   IVth-Vth Century.   10 x 28 cm.
PROVENANCE: Unknown.
BIBLIOGRAPHY: Unpublished.
LENT BY: *Mr. Dikran G. Kelekian.*

204.   SQUARE WITH FIGURES CLIMBING IN GRAPEVINE.   The vine
springs from a vase with dancing figures to right and left.   Border of
broken acanthus.   Purple and white tapestry weave.   IVth-Vth Century.
20.5 x 21.5 cm.
PROVENANCE: Unknown.
BIBLIOGRAPHY: Unpublished.
LENT BY: *Pratt Institute.*

205. **ROUNDEL WITH WARRIOR.** Dancing figure with shield and floating cloak in central medallion bordered by guilloche containing rosettes in reds and green. Tapestry-woven in colored wools and undyed linen. IVth-Vth Century. 23.3 x 21 cm.

PROVENANCE: Unknown.

BIBLIOGRAPHY: Unpublished.

LENT BY: *Mr. Dikran G. Kelekian.*

*206. **HEAD IN JEWELED FRAME.** Female portrait executed in naturalistic colors with black hair, on red ground. Border imitating gold frame set with jewels. Mounted with three additional smaller heads. IVth-Vth Century. 14.5 x 15 cm.

PROVENANCE: Unknown.

BIBLIOGRAPHY: Unpublished.

LENT BY: *Cooper Union Museum.*

A splendid example of the portrait heads so beloved of the late Classical weavers. Similar heads are in the Victoria and Albert Museum (from Akhmim. Kendrick, *Catalogue*, v. I, pp. 58 and 59, pl. XIV), in the Louvre (Pfister, *Tissus coptes*, pl. 21), and in the Berlin Museum (Wulff-Volbach, pl. 16). The last is practically identical with that from Cooper Union.

*207. **CLASSICAL FIGURES IN NICHES.** Four figures in niches supported by columns which have lost their functional quality. To the left, a shepherd, leaning on his staff; next a female figure, probably a nymph; then a vintner with sickle; finally another nymph. Purple-black wool and undyed linen tapestry weave. The border of conventionalized ivy leaves growing from urns is incorrectly assembled. Vth Century. 32.5 x 39.4 cm.

PROVENANCE: Unknown.

BIBLIOGRAPHY: Unpublished.

LENT BY: *Walters Art Gallery.*

*208. **GARLAND SUPPORTED BY GENII.** One of the most charming and spirited of Graeco-Roman textiles, in reddish purple wool and undyed linen. Tapestry weave in undyed woolen cloth. Vth Century. 40 x 10.5 cm.

PROVENANCE: Unknown.

BIBLIOGRAPHY: Unpublished.

LENT BY: *Textile Museum of the District of Columbia.*

*209.   FRAGMENT WITH CLASSICAL FIGURES.   Very finely tapestry-woven fragment, probably from front of elaborate tunic, showing nude musician (Pan?) with syrinx and dancing nymphs holding branches on tops of elaborate columns which spring from roundels (incomplete) containing animal motifs in jeweled borders.   Between the columns, winged Victories in Greek garments holding wreaths.   Badly stained; the only distinguishable color a deep blue.   Vth Century.   22.5 x 18.5 cm.

PROVENANCE: Unknown.

BIBLIOGRAPHY: Unpublished.

LENT BY: *Professor Vladimir G. Simkhovitch.*

   Cf. the Victories holding shields in the Palmyra frescoes (ill. in Dalton, *Byzantine art*, p. 277, fig. 168).

210.   DANCING FIGURES IN NICHES.   Semi-nude figures with floating draperies set in jeweled arches supported by columns.   Alternate figures carry shields.   Plant motifs suggest landscape.   Above, guilloche border and wider border ornamented with roundels; below, arched compartments with fruit baskets and urn.   Tapestry-woven in purple-black wool, with touches of color, and undyed linen.   Probably from front of tunic. Vth Century.   38 x 33 cm.

PROVENANCE: Unknown.

BIBLIOGRAPHY: Unpublished.

LENT BY: *Textile Museum of the District of Columbia.*

*211.   HERCULES.   Tapestry-woven in brilliant polychromy on red ground. Standing figure of Hercules with club and lion skin; to the right, a seated figure (Hera?), fold of veil in hand, and above, a reclining nymph pouring water from a vase.   Vth Century.   Diameter, 10.7 cm.

PROVENANCE: Unknown.   (Baron Collection)

BIBLIOGRAPHY: Riefstahl, R. M., Early textiles in the Cooper Union collection, in *Art in America*, v. III, 1915, p. 307, fig. 1 (opp. p. 302).

LENT BY: *Cooper Union Museum.*

   Probably symbolism of a mystery cult.

*212.   SQUARE WITH CHILD HOLDING DUCK.   Tapestry-woven in black wool and undyed linen, with touches of scarlet wool.   Vth Century. 13 x 12.5 cm.

PROVENANCE: Unknown.

BIBLIOGRAPHY: Unpublished.

Brooklyn Museum Collection.

*213. **RECLINING GENIUS WITH GOBLET.** Charmingly naïve rendering in colored wools on linen warp. The nude figure in tan outlined in red on blue background. Borders red and yellow. Vth Century. 19 x 31 cm.
PROVENANCE: Unknown.
BIBLIOGRAPHY: Unpublished.
LENT BY: *Philadelphia Museum of Art.*

*214. **ROUNDEL WITH PORTRAIT HEADS.** Very fine wool tapestry weave. Pale purplish-red ground, with design in red with tan shading outlined in undyed linen thread, combining late Classic and Sasanid motifs. Lions and birds are shown in opposite representation on either side of a tree which springs from an urn. Left and right of the center, delicately shaded portrait busts in medallions. Border of undulated vines with pomegranates. Vth-VIth Century. 20 x 20.5 cm.
PROVENANCE: Unknown.
BIBLIOGRAPHY: Unpublished.
LENT BY: *Textile Museum of the District of Columbia.*

*215. **ROUNDEL WITH PASIPHAE (?) AND THE BULL.** Charming composition showing semi-nude figure with floating draperies caressing bull; to the left another figure holding bowl and ewer (?). Tapestry weave of wool in lively colors and undyed linen. Vth-VIth Century. Diameter, 10 cm.
PROVENANCE: Antinoë. Excavations of the Egypt Exploration Society, 1913-1914.
BIBLIOGRAPHY: Unpublished.
Brooklyn Museum Collection.

216. **ROUNDEL WITH DANCING FIGURES.** Figures in central square. Portrait heads (?) in center of each side of square. Tapestry-woven in blue-black wool and undyed linen. Vth-VIth Century. Diameter, 8.5 cm.
PROVENANCE: Unknown. (Baron Collection)
BIBLIOGRAPHY: Unpublished.
LENT BY: *Cooper Union Museum.*

*217. **BANDS WITH MYTHOLOGICAL SCENES.** Tapestry-woven in brilliantly colored wools and undyed linen. Applied to plain linen cloth. Haloed goddess, semi-nude and with elaborate headdress, stands in compartment on red ground holding aloft flowers. At her feet, Eros and

Greek letters which seem to read Zoë (?), i.e., the personification of life, associated with Aphrodite. Remainder of bands filled with Nilotic scenes. On the right band, a Centaur playing on pipes and above, inscription for missing figure which may have been Octobrius (?). Vth-VIth Century. 53.4 x 53.4 cm.

PROVENANCE: Unknown.

BIBLIOGRAPHY: Unpublished.

LENT BY: *Boston Museum of Fine Arts.*

Professor Ranke informs us that the name Zoë was used by the Copts to designate Eve.

*218. ROUNDELS AND BANDS FROM TUNIC. Four roundels with, at left, seated figure nude to the waist, in right hand holding torch (?) and with left reaching to fruit basket in center foreground. From the right a winged figure approaches with offering of birds. Indications of landscape, including tree, in background. Two clavii with compartments containing figure draped and buskined, holding staff and making gesture of benediction (?); boys with birds; trees, etc. Two sleeve bands with center medallion showing seated figure making gesture of benediction (?). All figures with fair hair. Tapestry-woven in brilliantly colored wool and undyed linen on red ground. Vth-VIth Century. Size of frame, 74 x 55.5 cm.; diameter of roundels, 15.5 cm.

PROVENANCE: Unknown.

BIBLIOGRAPHY: Unpublished.

LENT BY: *Professor Vladimir G. Simkhovitch.*

Roundel only illustrated.

*219. SILK WITH SO-CALLED "DIOSCURI". Roundel of silk twill in white and light green on red ground. Two figures holding shield and spear stand on fluted column with a bull's head on base. To right and left, kneeling servants hold bulls; above, genii with bowls (?) and napkins. VIth Century. 10.25 x 10.25 cm..

PROVENANCE: Unknown.

BIBLIOGRAPHY: Unpublished.

LENT BY: *Textile Museum of the District of Columbia.*

Part of all-over design of connected roundels with plant motifs in the interstices. Cf. Lessing, v. I, pl. 12, for duplicate of this piece, found in tomb of St. Servatus, Maestricht, who died about 400 A.D. Probably a scene of sacrifice.

Roundel only illustrated.

*220. **SQUARE WITH PORTRAIT HEAD.** Boldly designed head framed in halo, bordered with Nilotic scenes (child with duck; child with bowl). Corner motifs with birds in medallions. Tapestry-woven in black and brilliant colors combined with undyed linen. VIth Century. Fragmentary, about 24 cm. square.

PROVENANCE: Unknown.

BIBLIOGRAPHY: Unpublished.

LENT BY: *Pratt Institute.*

Cf. head of similar style in combination with Nilotic figures in the Louvre (Pfister, *Tissus coptes,* pl. 30).

*221. **TAPESTRY WITH HORSEMEN.** Roundel in very fine tapestry weave of polychromed wool and undyed linen on mellowed rose-red ground. VIth Century. 23 x 27 cm.

PROVENANCE: Unknown.

BIBLIOGRAPHY: Unpublished.

LENT BY: *Textile Museum of the District of Columbia.*

Undoubtedly a copy of Sasanid silk. Cf. Lessing, v. I, pl. 8-10, for variations on this theme. Part of larger composition.

Roundel only illustrated.

*222. **SQUARE WITH NILOTIC SCENES.** In the corners, nereids on sea-monsters and nude children gathering lotus from a boat. Center and four border medallions with swimming children. Tapestry-woven in colored wools with touches of undyed linen thread against orange and yellow background. VIth Century. App. 30 cm. square.

PROVENANCE: Unknown.

BIBLIOGRAPHY: Unpublished.

LENT BY: *Mr. Kirkor Minassian.*

Analogous pieces in Louvre (Pfister, *Tissus coptes,* pl. 16-19. For a general discussion of Nilotic scenes see Pfister, Nil, Nilomètres et l'orientalisation du paysage hellénistique, in *Revue des arts asiatiques,* Paris, 1932, v. VII, p. 121-140).

223. **SQUARE WITH EUROPA AND THE BULL.** Figure in center of star-shaped medallion mounted on a bull. Borders of nymphs on sea-monsters. Brilliant polychromy in tapestry weave of wool and undyed linen. VIth Century. 27.5 cm. square.

PROVENANCE: Unknown.

BIBLIOGRAPHY: Unpublished.

LENT BY: *Pratt Institute.*

Europa with the bull was a favorite subject of late classic art. Technau, however, cautions against accepting all portrayals of female figures and bulls as illustrating the familiar myth; he recognizes in some an Oriental nature goddess, partly assimilated into Hellenistic mythology (*Jahrbuch der deutsches archeologisches institut*, v. 52, 1937, p. 76-103).

224. **ROUNDEL WITH PERSONAGES.** To the left, a seated figure; to the right, personage with offering (?). Fine tapestry weave on red ground. VIth Century. Diameter, 10.75 cm.
PROVENANCE: Unknown. (Baron Collection)
BIBLIOGRAPHY: Riefstahl, R. M., Early textiles in the Cooper Union collection, in *Art in America*, v. III, 1915, p. 307, fig. 10 (opp. p. 250).
LENT BY: *Cooper Union Museum.*

225. **REPEAT DESIGN OF SMALL SQUARES.** An unusual checkerboard pattern. Portrait heads in colors alternate with birds and floral sprays in small black-bordered squares (2 cm. square) with blue and yellow ground. Tapestry-woven. VIth Century. 24 x 16 cm.
PROVENANCE: Unknown.
BIBLIOGRAPHY: Unpublished.
LENT BY: *Pratt Institute.*

*226. **HORSEMAN.** Fragment, tapestry-woven in colored wools on yellow wool warps. Yellow ground. Remains of Coptic inscription. VIth-VIIth Century. 12 x 16 cm.
PROVENANCE: Unknown.
BIBLIOGRAPHY: Unpublished.
LENT BY: *Textile Museum of the District of Columbia.*
The inscription, ". . . pnote," can be the end of the well-known Coptic name, Papnute (sometimes Paphnute), and as such may refer to a famous monk and ascetic of the fourth century.

*227. **SILK EMBROIDERED ROUNDEL.** Embroidery in satin stitch on linen cloth. Central motif of animals in opposite representation on either side of a highly conventionalized tree, around which are swimming figures, fish, floral motifs, animals crudely designed. Outer border of heart-shaped leaves. Blue and green on yellowed background. VIth-VIIth Century. Diameter, 24 cm.
PROVENANCE: Unknown.
BIBLIOGRAPHY: Unpublished.

72

LENT BY: *Mr. Kirkor Minassian.*

Such silk-embroidered roundels, indeed embroidered fabrics in any materials, are much rarer than woven fabrics. The Victoria and Albert Museum possesses several examples with Biblical scenes (Kendrick, *Catalogue*, v. III, chapter 5). A square with an angel similarly embroidered (in wool?) is in Athens (Apostolaki, p. 179, fig. 152; dated IVth-Vth Century). Cf. also a specimen from the collection of the Metropolitan Museum illustrated in this catalogue.

*228. **SILK EMBROIDERED ROUNDEL.** Scene of combat between two horsemen, with lion or dog in foreground, executed in satin-stitch on linen cloth. VIth-VIIth Century. 20 x 13.5 cm.
PROVENANCE: Akhmim.
BIBLIOGRAPHY: Metropolitan Museum of Art, *Catalogue of Textiles*, 1916, No. 53.
LENT BY: *Metropolitan Museum of Art.*

229. **BORDER WITH GENII.** Flying figures alternate with a horseman who holds a whip. Between them are hares. Wool and cotton tapestry weave on purple ground. VIth-VIIth Century (?).
PROVENANCE: Unknown.
BIBLIOGRAPHY: Unpublished.
LENT BY: *Textile Museum of the District of Columbia.*

This piece is said to show cotton in the weft, while the warps are wool. This fact arouses many interesting speculations as to date and provenance, cotton being all but unknown in Egyptian textiles of the earlier period.

230. **MAN FIGHTING LION.** Roundel in imitation of silk weave, tapestry-woven in colored wools and undyed linen thread on red ground scattered with floral motifs. VIth-VIIth Century. 18.7 x 15.5 cm.
PROVENANCE: Unknown.
BIBLIOGRAPHY: Unpublished.
LENT BY: *Mr. Dikran G. Kelekian.*

HANGINGS AND FRAGMENTS OF HANGINGS

*231.   TAPESTRY-WOVEN HEAD.   Fine late Classic design in naturalistic colors showing skilful use of hatching in producing modeling.   IIIrd-IVth Century.   16 x 12 cm.

PROVENANCE: Unknown.

BIBLIOGRAPHY: Weibel Adele C., A fragment of Hellenistic wool tapestry, in Detroit Institute of Arts, *Bulletin*, v. XV, 1936, p. 84-85.

LENT BY: *Detroit Institute of Arts.*

Mrs. Weibel in her article in the Detroit *Bulletin* attributes this splendid piece probably to Syria. Whatever its provenance, it is one of the very fine specimens extant of the Graeco-Roman weaver's art. Its size, about one-half life size, makes it probable that it once formed part of a hanging.

*232.   CHILD WITH DUCK.   Figure of late Classic design.   Nude save for scarf and high black boots, holding duck in right hand and branch (?) in left.   On red ground with scattered floral motifs.   Tapestry-woven in colored wools with black outlines.   Background in small part wrongly assembled in the modern mounting.   IVth Century.   35 x 37 cm.

PROVENANCE: Unknown.

BIBLIOGRAPHY: Kelekian, *Important documents of Coptic art*, New York, [1929].

LENT BY: *Mr. Dikran G. Kelekian.*

233.   WINGED GENIUS.   Fragment of hanging tapestry-woven in black and colored wool into undyed linen cloth.   Below, ornamental motifs in colored wools.   IVth Century.   56 x 34.7 cm.

PROVENANCE: Unknown.

BIBLIOGRAPHY: Unpublished.

LENT BY: *Mr. Dikran G. Kelekian.*

*234.   SCENE WITH WARRIOR.   Fragment of large hanging, tapestry-woven in colored wools and undyed linen.   Two large roundels show against a red ground a warrior, in the armor of a Roman soldier, arrested in the act of slaughter; his intended victim clings to his knee.   Roundels set on blue background with design delicately delineated in darker blue.   Wide border with conventionalized floral motifs.   IVth-Vth Century.   101.5 x 53.7 cm.

PROVENANCE: Unknown.

74

BIBLIOGRAPHY: Unpublished.
LENT BY: *Mr. H. Kevorkian.*
    Detail only illustrated.

*235.   THE JUDGMENT OF PARIS.   Part of a tapestry-woven hanging in colored wools and undyed linen thread, showing brilliantly colored figures against a background, the upper part of which is red, the lower part green with "mille fleur" decoration.   The figure of Athena stands to the left.   Next to her, the lower part of another female figure.   A bearded head has been wrongly inserted as part of this figure.   The cadeuces of a vanished Hermes between them has been taken from another part of the composition.   Border of palmette flowers on white ground.   At top, in Greek letters: to the left, "Athena" and, to the right, "Paris".   IVth-Vth Century.   77.5 x 82 cm.

PROVENANCE: Unknown.

BIBLIOGRAPHY: Unpublished.

LENT BY: *Mr. H. Kevorkian.*

    Probably part of a larger composition, showing Athena, Hera, Aphrodite, Hermes and Paris.   Though what remains has been to a large extent incorrectly assembled, this is an extremely interesting specimen of Graeco-Roman weaving, with a subtlety of color and shading that had to be re-learned by medieval craftsmen.

*236.   WINGED GENIUS WITH FRUIT BASKET.   Late Classical design in naturalistic colors.   Looped technique.   IVth-Vth Century.   37 x 30 cm.

PROVENANCE: Unknown.

BIBLIOGRAPHY: Unpublished.

Brooklyn Museum Collection.

    Figures such as these, probably from large hangings, are comparatively rare. Cf. figure of boy in Victoria and Albert Museum (Kendrick, *Catalogue*, p. 49, pl. X) and, especially, the examples in Berlin (Wulff-Volbach, pls. 1 and 39).

*237.   MASK IN LOOPED TECHNIQUE.   Boldly designed in colored wools, against a background with stepped lozenges also in looping.   The head has not been woven with the background but has been set into it, probably in very modern times.   IVth-Vth Century.

PROVENANCE: Unknown.

BIBLIOGRAPHY: Unpublished.

Brooklyn Museum Collection.

Though this is a "made up" piece, there is evidence that similar disembodied heads, or masks, were used as ornaments for large hangings (cf. one of similar style from Akhmim in Victoria and Albert Museum: Kendrick, *Catalogue*, v. 1, p. 49, pl. X). Masks, mounted similarly to the present specimen, are in the Simkhovitch and Kelekian collections, New York, the latter illustrated in Kelekian, *Important documents of Coptic art* [1929].

*238.   HANGING WITH BACCHIC FIGURES.   Roundels formed by intertwined vines enclose symbolic heads representing nymphs, Pan with goat horns, and other characters of the Bacchic festivals.   Of skilful weave and fine polychromy.   Tapestry-woven in wool and undyed linen.   Vth Century.   91 x 125 cm.

PROVENANCE: Probably Antinoë.

BIBLIOGRAPHY: Winlock, H. E., A Roman tapestry and a Roman rug, in *Bulletin of the Metropolitan Museum of Art*, v. 27, 1932, p. 157, fig. 1.

LENT BY: *Metropolitan Museum of Art.*

239.   HANGING WITH LATTICE DESIGN.   Tapestry-woven in colored wools on linen wrap.   Center field with all-over design of lozenges formed by leaves with floral rosette at corners, which contain birds, floral sprays and portrait heads on red ground.   Border of portrait heads in peaked caps on blue.   Vth-VIth Century.   70 x 122 cm.

PROVENANCE: Unknown.

BIBLIOGRAPHY: Unpublished.

LENT BY: *Textile Museum of the District of Columbia.*

Such lattices are a familiar feature of later Egyptian textile design.   Similar patterns, obviously derived from textiles, are on the Bawit frescoes.

*240.   ROUNDEL WITH HORSE.   Realistic rendering of a riderless horse, tapestry-woven in colors against a red background with landscape suggested by a tree.   Border of heart-shaped motifs.   Left side partly rewoven with old thread.   Vth-VIth Century.   39.6 x 44.8 cm.

PROVENANCE: Unknown.

BIBLIOGRAPHY: Unpublished.

LENT BY: *Walters Art Gallery.*

Probably part of a large hanging.   For another example see Pierce, Hayford, and Tyler, Royall, *L'Art byzantin*, t. II, pl. 57 a.

*241.   HANGING WITH LEOPARDS.   Tapestry-woven in colored wool and undyed linen thread on green wool warps.   Heraldic leopards on either side of a conventionalized tree are shown in six large roundels on red ground, which are placed against a green ground ornamented with wavy lines. Between the roundels are floral rosettes, of the style frequently found as scatter motifs on hangings. Border of roundels containing, alternately, floral designs and very spirited horses. Vth-VIth Century. 155 x 110 cm.

PROVENANCE: Unknown.

BIBLIOGRAPHY: Unpublished.

LENT BY: *Textile Museum of the District of Columbia.*

Another wool weave inspired by Sasanid silks. For analogous silk weave with similar leopards, cf. Lessing, v. I, pl. 2a.

*242. HANGING WITH WHITE HORSES. Remarkably lively design of three friezes of white horses held by attendants, tapestry-woven in wool of fine colors on red ground. Friezes separated by floral bands; floral sprays in background. Border of heads and heart-shaped flowers. Vth-VIth Century. 82 x 110 cm.

PROVENANCE: Unknown.

BIBLIOGRAPHY: Unpublished.

LENT BY: *Textile Museum of the District of Columbia.*

The attendants furnish an interesting document of costume. A piece with all-over design of stylized heads almost identical with those of the border is in Kansas City; another is in Lyon.

Two friezes only illustrated.

*243.   HEAD OF SAINT THEODORE.   Two fragments probably from the same large hanging.   One with the head of a haloed saint very skilfully executed in colors.   The second with remains of a jeweled border and part of an inscription legible as O AGI(OS) THEOD(OROS), i.e., Saint Theodore.   Vth Century.   Fragment with head, 32 x 45 cm.   Fragment with inscription, 48 x 37 cm.

PROVENANCE: Unknown.

BIBLIOGRAPHY: Tyler, W. R., Fragments of an early Christian tapestry, in *Bulletin of the William Hayes Fogg Art Museum*, v. 9, 1939, p. 2-13.

LENT BY: *William Hayes Fogg Art Museum.*

Fragment with head illustrated.

*244.   FRAGMENT WITH CROSS.   Piece of narrow ribbon, silk and linen on silk warp, with cross tapestry-woven in brown and gold.   Vth-VIth Century.   4.5 x 4 cm.

PROVENANCE: Antinoë.   Excavation of Egypt Exploration Society, 1913-14.

BIBLIOGRAPHY: Unpublished.

Brooklyn Museum Collection.

*245.   ROUNDEL WITH ACROSTIC.   Inscribed with cross-shaped acrostic in Greek letters, white on purple, reading, horizontally, "life" and, vertically, "light".   Vth-VIth Century.   Diameter, 3.2 cm.

PROVENANCE: Antinoë.   Excavation of Egypt Exploration Society, 1913-14.

BIBLIOGRAPHY: Unpublished.

Brooklyn Museum Collection.

*246.   ANTLERED DEER.   Very fine tapestry weave in delicate polychromy with black outlines.   Vth-VIth Century.   5.5 x 5.5 cm.

PROVENANCE: Antinoë.   Excavation of Egypt Exploration Society, ,1913-14.

BIBLIOGRAPHY: Unpublished.

Brooklyn Museum Collection.

The stag is a familiar motif of ancient Near Eastern art, both of the Christian and pre-Christian period.   Cf. pottery from Yorgan Tepa, Mesopotamia, with similar stags, of the IIIrd Century A.D.   (Erich, Robert W., The later cultures at Yorgan Tepa, in Starr, F. S., *Nuzi*. . . Cambridge, Mass., 1939, v. 1, p. 566-568; v. II, pl. 137).   Features of this textile might assign it to a Mesopotamian origin, including the use of what seems to be cotton thread in the blue.

*247. **JEWELED CROSS.** Tapestry-woven into linen cloth to simulate jewels on red ground. Vth-VIth Century. 14.5 x 16 cm.
PROVENANCE: Unknown.
BIBLIOGRAPHY: Unpublished.
LENT BY: *Pratt Institute.*

    Cf. crosses from Akhmim in Victoria and Albert Museum (Kendrick, *Catalogue,* v. II, p. 14, pl. III).

248. **BORDER WITH ORANS.** Coarse tapestry weave in purple wool and undyed linen. Ovals reminiscent of vine motif with tendrils attached containing, alternately, crudely drawn figure, in attitude of orans, and rosette motif. Vth-VIth Century. 50 x 10.5 cm.
PROVENANCE: Unknown.
BIBLIOGRAPHY: *Brooklyn museum quarterly,* v. XVI, 1929, p. 52.
LENT BY: *Pratt Institute.*

*249. **COPTIC SAINT.** Female saint as orans in brilliantly colored looping on plain linen. To the right a candelabrum. Last two letters of Coptic inscription, seemingly "L" and "A" (St. Thekla?). Vth-VIth Century. 38 x 33.5 cm.
PROVENANCE: Unknown.
BIBLIOGRAPHY: Unpublished.
LENT BY: *Textile Museum of the District of Columbia.*

250. **ORANS IN NICHE.** An orans in jeweled niche, with cross over his head. Looping in colored wools on plain linen cloth. Interesting polychromy, feet and hands red; face in red, yellow and blue. Vth-VIth Century. 39 x 40 cm.
PROVENANCE: Unknown.
BIBLIOGRAPHY: *Pennsylvania museum bulletin,* no. 69, October, 1921, p. 11-15.
LENT BY: *Philadelphia Museum of Art.*

*251. **PERSONAGE IN A CHARIOT.** Vividly colored wool tapestry roundel showing highly stylized figure in a chariot drawn by bulls. "Tree of life" in background. VIth Century. Diameter, 12 cm.
PROVENANCE: Unknown.
BIBLIOGRAPHY: Unpublished.
Brooklyn Museum Collection.

    The crossed nimbus inspires the speculation as to whether this may be an unorthodox representation of the Ascension, based on earlier, purely pagan representation of divinities in chariots drawn by bulls.

*252.   LARGE ROUNDEL WITH HORSEMAN.   Haloed figure with flowing mantle and carrying sceptre and ring.   At his feet are lions, and on either side, figures in grotesque postures.   Floral sprays and traces of letters in background.   Border with plant forms.   Tapestry-woven in colored wools and undyed linen thread against a red background into plain linen cloth.   VIth Century.   23.5 x 21 cm.

PROVENANCE: Unknown. (Baron Collection)

BIBLIOGRAPHY: Worcester Museum catalogue, *The Dark Ages*, Worcester, 1937, no. 142; Riefstahl, R. M., Early textiles in the Cooper Union collection, in *Art in America*, v. III, 1915, p. 308, fig. 2 (opp. p. 302).

LENT BY: *Cooper Union Museum.*

While the hunting horseman, a familiar figure of Sasanid silks, is sometimes literally repeated in wool variations from Egypt, the motif has here evidently been transformed into a rider saint.   A very similar roundel, but with a different border, is in the Victoria and Albert Museum (Kendrick, *Catalogue*, v. 3, p. 24, pl. XIII).   For discussion of rider saint see Strzygowski, Josef, Der koptische Reiterheilige und der heilige Georg, in *Zeitschrift für ägyptische Sprache*, v. 40, 1902, p. 49-60.

*253.   SACRIFICE OF ISAAC.   Sleeve band from a tunic, tapestry-woven in colored wools and undyed linen into a coarse linen cloth.   The band is divided into three panels.   In the central panel, on orange ground, Abraham is shown, knife in hand, holding his nude son by the hair. From the left corner, the hand of God reaches down to arrest the sacrifice. At the feet of the patriarch is the ram ready for substitution.   In the background is a suggestion of a tree and scattered Coptic letters.   The end panels with all-over design of lozenges containing floral motifs and birds on red ground.   VIth Century.   29 x 14.5 cm.

PROVENANCE: Unknown. (Baron Collection)

BIBLIOGRAPHY: Worcester Museum catalogue, *The Dark Ages*, Worcester, 1937, no. 141.   Riefstahl, R. M., Early tapestries in the Cooper Union collection, in *Art in America*, v. III, 1915, p. 300, fig. 12 (opp. p. 250).

LENT BY: *Cooper Union Museum.*

A number of tapestry weaves with Biblical subjects, often difficult to identify, are known (Kendrick, *Catalogue*, v. 3, p. 36 ff).   This one has the merit of being unmistakable, and is very interesting in connection with a wood panel of later date in the present exhibition.   According to Dalton, the scenes of the sacrifice of Isaac have an added symbolic Christian significance of deliverance and redemption (British Museum, *Guide to the Early Christian and Byzantine Antiquities*, London, 1921, p. 86).   Almost an exact duplicate in Lyon, Musée

Historique des Tissus (*Tapisseries et étoffes coptes,* published by H. Ernst, Paris, n. d., pl. 17; and Grüneisen, *Caracteristiques,* pl. XXIV).

254. PART OF GREEN WOOLEN TUNIC. Tunic-front of wool with nap, with applied tapestry-woven bands in brilliant colors, showing haloed saint in elaborate costume and headdress, his hand upraised in blessing, together with animals and trees of Persian style. Borders of undulated vines, yellow on black. VIth Century. 80 x 27 cm.
PROVENANCE: Unknown.
BIBLIOGRAPHY: Unpublished.
Brooklyn Museum Collection.

*255. FRONT OF TUNIC. Yellow wool with tapestry-woven bands showing nymphs and sea-monsters, yellow on brown. At neck, in colors, jeweled chain with cross and, in V formed by chain, a crude, nude female figure in dancing posture, with elaborate headdress and upraised hands holding heart-shaped red objects. VIth Century. 33 x 113 cm.
PROVENANCE: Unknown.
BIBLIOGRAPHY: Unpublished.
Brooklyn Museum Collection.

Strzygowski speculates as to whether this combination of cross and dancing figure may not be a Gnostic symbol.

*256. LANCE-SHAPED ORNAMENT. Stag in foliage. The stag, in soft natural tones, on a background of leaves against a green ground. Tapestry weave in colored wools and undyed linen in linen cloth. VIth Century. 15.5 x 16.5 cm.
PROVENANCE: Unknown.
BIBLIOGRAPHY: Unpublished.
LENT BY: *Textile Museum of the District of Columbia.*

*257. SAINT, STAG AND SERPENT. Wool and linen tapestry weave in colors on red ground. To the left, from a tree, a serpent fascinates a stag, which looks up from the left foreground; to the right is a saint, haloed and bearing a palm-branch (a martyr?). Remains of inscription. VIth Century. 22 x 32.5 cm.
PROVENANCE: Unknown.
BIBLIOGRAPHY: Unpublished.
LENT BY: *Textile Museum of the District of Columbia.*

Cf. the stag of the Bawit frescoes, in the coils of a serpent (Chapel XVII. See Clédat, La monastère et nécropole de Baouit, pls. XLVIII-XLIX, in *Memoirs de l'Institut français. . .* t. XII, Cairo, 1904).

The story of the antagonism of stag and serpent is old in Greek legend. It is repeated, with its Christian symbolism, by the Physiologus, or Natural Philosopher, an anonymous author who wrote, perhaps in Alexandria, perhaps in Caesarea, sometime between the IInd and IVth Century A. D. He explains the simile of David, "as the hart panteth after the water-brooks," by saying that the stag is always thirsty as a result of eating snakes, his enemies, and adds that, as the stag kills the snake, so the Lord kills the great dragon, that is, the Devil, by the celestial waters, the virtuous doctrines of Christ. As the serpent cannot approach the stag, so the Devil cannot approach the person filled with the word of God.

*258. ST. MICHAEL AND THE DRAGON. Plain compound silk twill with design in white (ecru) on purple-blue ground. In the lower compartment, the saint, cross in hand, thrusts a spear into the mouth of the dragon; in the upper, an animal attacked by a bird of prey. VIth Century. 18 x 6.5 cm.
PROVENANCE: Probably Akhmim.
BIBLIOGRAPHY: Unpublished.
LENT BY: *Philadelphia Museum of Art.*
    A duplicate, less well preserved, in the Victoria and Albert Museum (Kendrick, *Catalogue,* v. I, p. 81, pl. XXV).

259. BAND WITH COPTIC INSCRIPTION. From tunic. Very debased design of Nilotic scenes tapestry-woven in colored wool on red ground. At intervals, medallions with nude figures and animals on blue ground. Along one edge of the border, the inscription "Apa Isidore" with cross at either end. VIth-VIIth Century. 57 x 41 cm.
PROVENANCE: Unknown.
BIBLIOGRAPHY: Unpublished.
LENT BY: *Mr. Dikran G. Kelekian.*

*260. SAINTS (?) WITH STAFF AND GLOBE. Tapestry-woven frieze of brilliantly colored figures separated by tree motifs on a blue ground. VIth-VIIth Century. 61 x 16.5 cm.
PROVENANCE: Unknown.
BIBLIOGRAPHY: Pfister, Étoffes coptes, in *Cahiers d'Art,* v. V, 1930, p. 28-30.
LENT BY: *Textile Museum of the District of Columbia.*
    Other examples of this type of design, with wild colors, the figures with pinched waists and bouffant skirts, are known. Pfister believes that they show not merely Persian influence, but the influence of a barbaric pre-Islamic Arabia.

261. **FRAGMENT OF TUNIC.** Clavii with haloed saint and lamb or doe by tree, ending in finials with haloed heads. Tapestry weave in vivid wools and undyed linen on red ground in yellow woolen cloth. VIth-VIIth Century. 34 x 65.5 cm.

PROVENANCE: Unknown.

BIBLIOGRAPHY: Unpublished.

LENT BY: *Textile Museum of the District of Columbia.*

A very similar piece in the Louvre (Pfister, *Tissus coptes,* Pl. 1).

262. **LARGE COVERLET WITH INSCRIPTION.** Looped linen with bands at ends and four large squares in center field tapestry-woven in purple wool with design of interlacing and octagonal stars in undyed linen. The bands end in crosses with smaller crosses in the angles. Broad plain band at either end bears Coptic inscription in purple flanked, at the top, by arches containing "Greek" and "ankh" crosses, in blue and purple, at the bottom, by blue and purple "ankh" cross elaborately developed into globe and star pattern and, at the extreme edge, by "Greek" cross with crosses in the angles. The tapestry-woven bands are separated from the body of the textile by rows of red, green and blue looping; the ends are finished by woolen cords. VIth-VIIth Century. 221.5 cm. x 147 cm.

PROVENANCE: Unknown.

BIBLIOGRAPHY: Unpublished.

LENT BY: *Mr. H. Kevorkian.*

An important piece. Dr. Walter Federn distinguishes the names "Sarapion" and "Thekla" as part of the inscription. The whole inscription probably reads "K(ristos) M(aria) G(enna) Sarapion Thekla," i.e., "Christ, son of Mary. Sarapion. Thekla."

263. **LARGE RESIST-DYED HANGING.** Linen cloth with design of central cross and four smaller crosses in medallions against an all-over design of jeweled arches containing flower shrub. Ground blue; design reserved in natural linen (browned), with details in blue and purplish red (faded). VIth-VIIth Century. 270 x 131 cm.

PROVENANCE: Said to be Bawit.

BIBLIOGRAPHY: Unpublished.

LENT BY: *Mr. H. Kevorkian.*

Dyed cloths must have existed in Egypt, at least from the first century of our era; for the process is described in detail by Pliny. A few fragments of hangings with Biblical scenes in this technique are known, and one remarkable specimen showing the cortege of Bacchus is in the Musée Guimet. The specimen here shown has the distinction of being practically complete and is, so far as I know, unique among the early printed textiles preserved in showing a purely ornamental design.

*264.   STOLE OR ORARION WITH APOSTLES. Three fragments of tapestry-woven stole with figures of Jesus, bearded, with a cruciferous nimbus, Mary, as orans, and the apostles Mark, Thomas, Matthew, Bartholemew and Simon (?), in colored wools and undyed linen. The figures are designated by names in Greek characters; the inscription "Philip" remains, though the figure is missing. Crosses and a conventionalized tree are interspersed with the figures. VIIth-VIIIth Century. 5 cm. x 174 cm. total length.

PROVENANCE: Unknown.

BIBLIOGRAPHY: Unpublished.

LENT BY: *Professor Vladimir G. Simkhovitch.*

For the use and character of Coptic stole and orarion, see Butler, A. J., *The ancient Coptic churches of Egypt,* Oxford, 1884, p. 127-143.

265. **CHILD'S TUNIC.** Inlaid geometric ornament in colored wools. Vth-VIth Century.
PROVENANCE: Unknown.
BIBLIOGRAPHY: Unpublished.
Brooklyn Museum Collection.

266. **TUNIC WITH CROSS.** Linen, with remains of applied tapestry-woven ornament of Classical design in black wool and undyed linen. Cross embroidered in scarlet, front and back. Tuck for girdle-cord. Vth-VIth Century.
PROVENANCE: Unknown.
BIBLIOGRAPHY: Unpublished.
Brooklyn Museum Collection.

For discussion of styles of tunics during the Coptic period see Pfister, *Tissus coptes,* p. 2, with diagrams; Kendrick in *Burlington Magazine,* v. 32, 1918, p. 145; Dimand, *Ornamentik,* p. 10-22; Pfister, La décoration des étoffes d'Antinoë, in *Revue des arts asiatiques,* v. V, 1928, p. 215-243.

267. **COPTIC TUNIC.** A well preserved example of a complete tunic in yellow wool rep ornamented with tapestry-woven bands in dark blue with touches of pale purple, showing figures in niches and, at the neck, an especially interesting design of a figure between griffins. VIIth Century.
PROVENANCE: Unknown.
BIBLIOGRAPHY: Unpublished.
LENT BY: *Mme. Marguerite Mallon.*

The motif of the figure between griffins may represent the legendary journey of Kai Khosrau or Alexander the Great to Heaven, a subject of Near Eastern folklore and art which was carried over into the Mohammedan period and found its way into medieval Europe. Iconographically, it probably goes back to a period before the time of either king. (Cf. Loomis, R. S., Alexander the Great's celestial journey, in *Burlington Magazine,* v. 32, 1918, p. 136-140, 177-185. Also Herzfeld, Ernst, Der Thron des Khosro, in *Jahrb. d. preuss. kunstsamml.,* v. 41, Berlin, 1920, p. 1-24, 103-147).

268. ANIMALS IN VINE SCROLLS. Very impressionistic rendering of familiar motif in purple and green wool and undyed linen tapestry-woven into coarse linen cloth with linen looping. VIIth-IXth Century. 88.5 x 36 cm.

PROVENANCE: Unknown.

BIBLIOGRAPHY: Unpublished.

LENT BY: *Textile Museum of the District of Columbia.*

This familiar motif of earlier Coptic art is also found in wood-carving of of the Islamic period.

269. DRINKING PERSONAGES. Highly stylized figures holding goblets, with birds and floral motifs in the background. Brightly colored wool tapestry weave on black ground. Wool warps. Of the Islamic period, with derivatives from the earlier textile style. VIIth-IXth Century. 10.5 x 68 cm.

PROVENANCE: Unknown.

BIBLIOGRAPHY: Unpublished.

LENT BY: *Textile Museum of the District of Columbia.*

270. BAND WITH ZIG-ZAG ORNAMENT. Wool tapestry weave in vivid coloring on red ground. Yellow wool warps. Zig-zags and background ornamented with geometrized figures of animals and birds. VIIth-IXth Century. 12 x 52 cm.

PROVENANCE: Unknown.

BIBLIOGRAPHY: Unpublished.

LENT BY: *Textile Museum of the District of Columbia.*

This textile, of the Islamic period, carries on the earlier weaving tradition and some of the familiar motifs—birds, lions, etc. (Cf. Kühnel, Ernst, La tradition copte dans les tissus musulmans, in *Bulletin de la Société d'archéologie copte*, t. IV, Cairo, 1938, p. [79]-89, pl. I). The Brooklyn Museum possesses fragments of two similar borders (not exhibited).

*271. SEATED SULTAN. Figure in white garment with colored spots, on blue ground. VIIIth-IXth Century. 26 x 40 cm.

PROVENANCE: Unknown.

BIBLIOGRAPHY: Unpublished.

LENT BY: *Textile Museum of the District of Columbia.*

Comparable with the figures on Fatimid pottery.

ILLUSTRATIONS

NOTE

Each illustration is designated
by the catalogue number of the object.
There are no plate numbers.

1

2

3

4

5

6

7

9

10

11

12

13

18

18

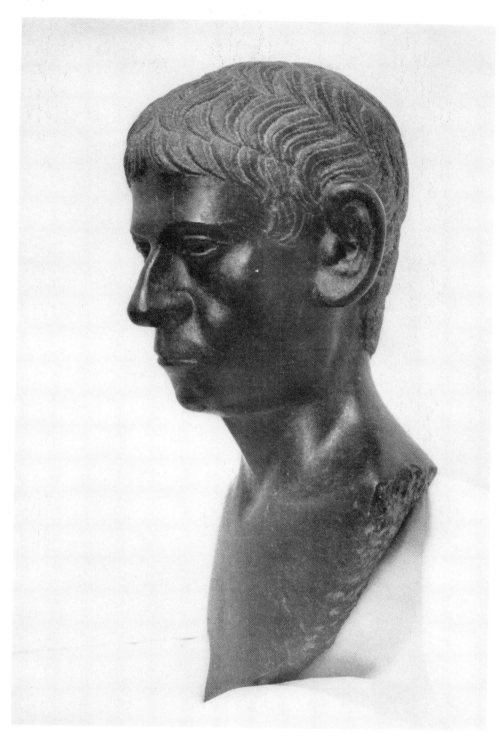

20

28

24

25

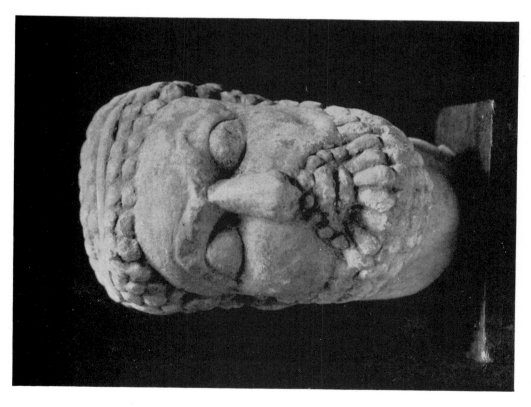

29

30

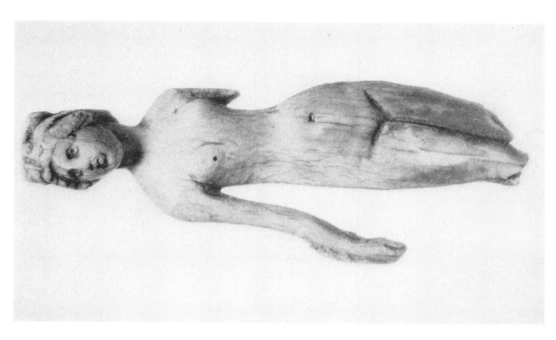

101

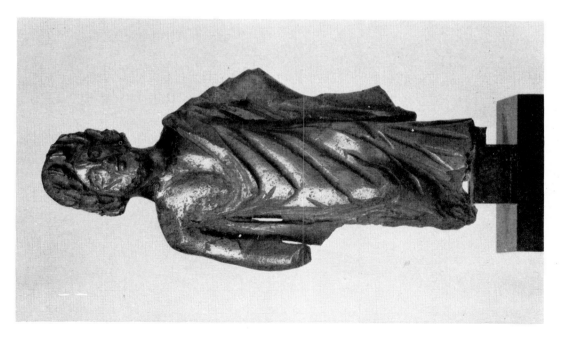

32

33

34

35

36

38

39

40

64

41

42

44

45

57

48

49

53

52

65

66

70

71

73

100

78

80

81

82

85

85

86

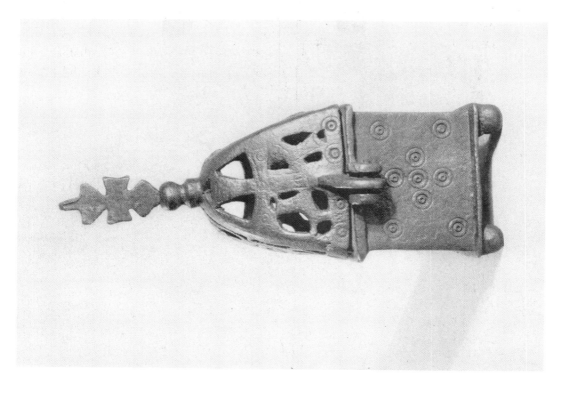

87

87

89

90

91

93

99

95

103

96

106

98

117

105

105

107

108

120

124

125

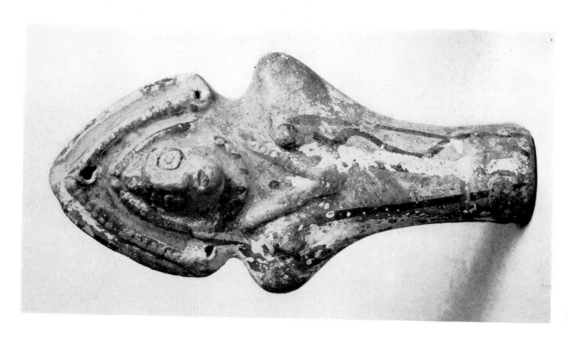

127

126

132

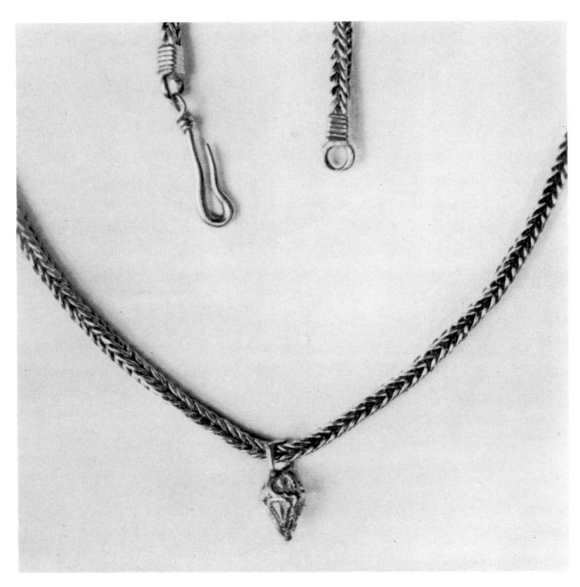

130

131

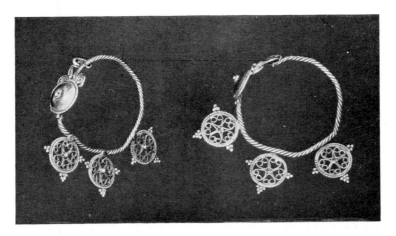

136

138

140

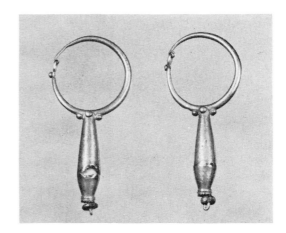

139

141 & 142

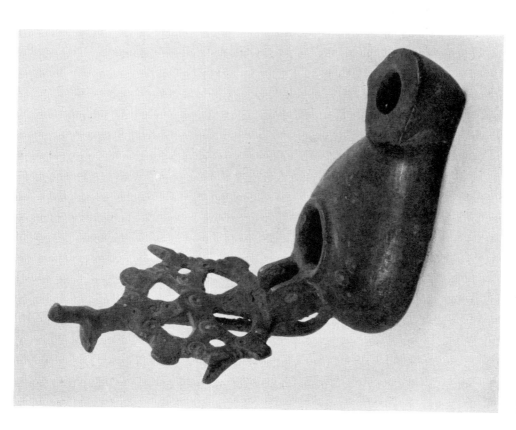

83

146

145

158

148

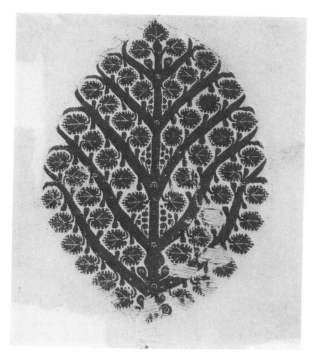

154

152

153

163

212

159

190

193

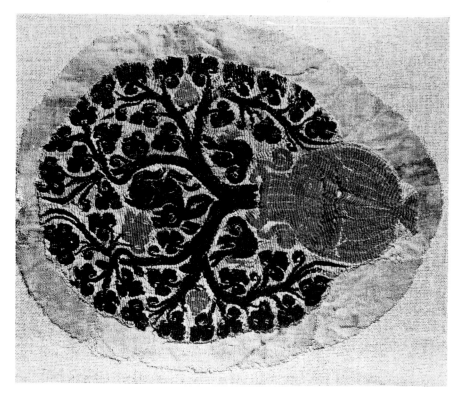

157

170

181

192

172

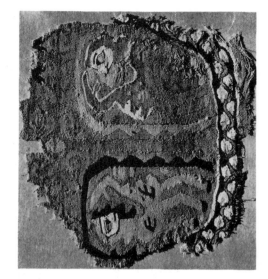

174

176

175

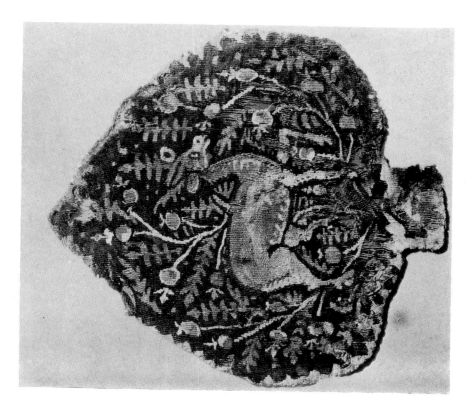

256

177

182

183

184

185

173

187

195

189

201

211

191

207

214

258

251

178

218

215

161

206

213

220

208

209

217

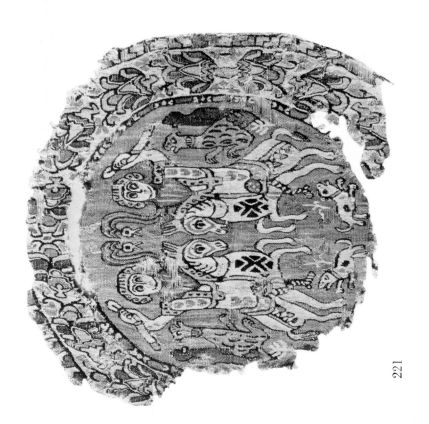

221

219

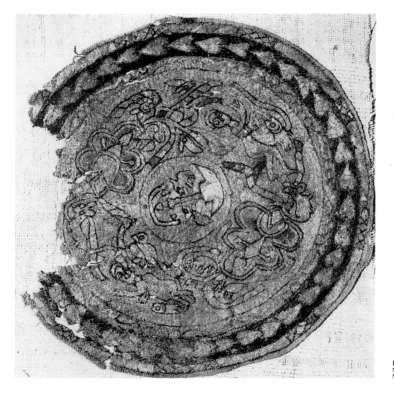

227

222

260

271

226

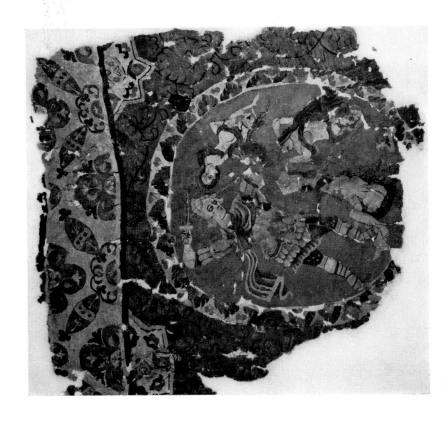

234

228

232

240

231

235

236

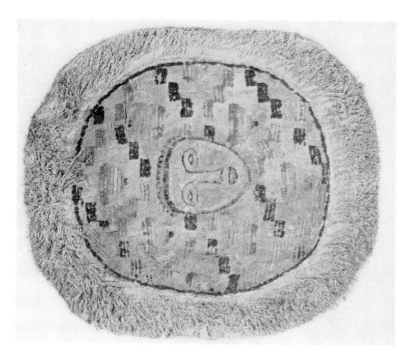

237

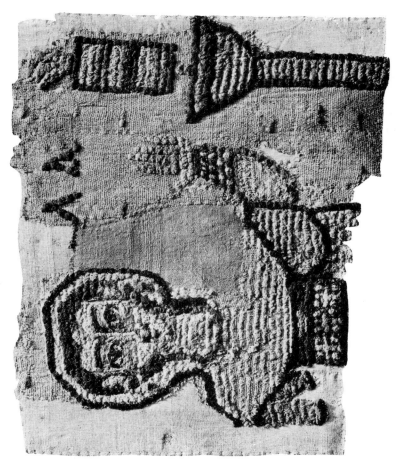

249

238

243

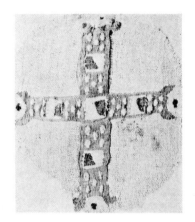

247

246

245

264

244

253

252

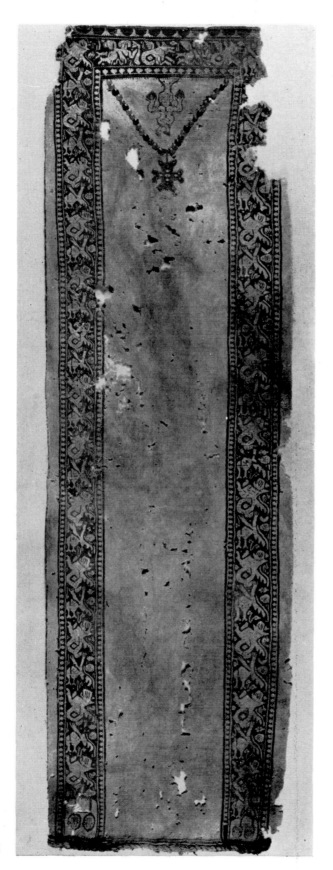

255

257

NOTE ON ILLUSTRATIONS

The following illustrations are reproduced from photographs made by the Brooklyn Museum Studio, under the direction of Herman de Wetter, A.R.P.S.

Nos. 2, 3, 10, 11, 18, 30, 33, 35, 36, 41, 42, 48, 49, 50, 57, 58, 59, 60, 67, 70, 71, 78, 80, 83, 86, 89, 91, 96, 99, 100, 103, 120, 124, 125, 126, 127, 130, 132, 136, 138, 139, 140, 141, 142, 145, 146, 157, 158, 159, 163, 170, 172, 173, 185, 190, 191, 192, 193, 209, 212, 215, 218, 220, 222, 227, 232, 234, 235, 236, 237, 244, 245, 246, 247, 251, 255, 264.

All other illustrations are reproduced through the courtesy of the owners of the objects.